The Six-Minute Entrepreneur

52 Short Lessons for Long-Term Business Success

Sara Davies

torva

TRANSWORLD PUBLISHERS

Penguin Random House, One Embassy Gardens,
8 Viaduct Gardens, London SW11 7BW
www.penguin.co.uk

Transworld is part of the Penguin Random House group of companies
whose addresses can be found at global.penguinrandomhouse.com

Penguin
Random House
UK

First published in Great Britain in 2025 by Torva
an imprint of Transworld Publishers

A CIP catalogue record for this book
is available from the British Library.

ISBNs
9781911709633 hb

Typeset in 12/18pt Sabon LT Pro by Jouve (UK), Milton Keynes
Printed and bound in Great Britain by Clays Ltd, Elcograf S.p.A.

The authorized representative in the EEA is Penguin Random House Ireland,
Morrison Chambers, 32 Nassau Street, Dublin D02 YH68.

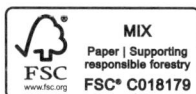

MIX
Paper | Supporting
responsible forestry
FSC
www.fsc.org   FSC® C018179

For Alex and Jason. I might have some amazing stories to tell, but *they* are the true storytellers!

Contents

Foreword

I often get asked the question: 'What are the ingredients for success?' There is a long answer and a short answer. Let's get the short answer out of the way here, then we can talk about the long answer over the rest of this book.

The short answer is that there are lots of things that you need to be successful, but if you're whittling them down to three cornerstone qualities, you need to have passion, vision and drive. It really doesn't matter how great your product is, or how amazing your business plan looks on paper; if you lack these three ingredients, you're probably heading for failure.

Passion has been a key element behind my success. Moments after I came off-air following my début appearance presenting my products on a shopping channel in the United States, I went to read the viewer feedback. A woman had said, 'I didn't understand a word she was saying but she seemed so happy, I wanted one anyway!'

I also present on shopping channels in Germany, and

Sara Davies

I don't even speak German. Customers still buy from me! Passion is irresistible, in any language.

In any new business, it is also essential that you have a clear *vision* of where you want to be. You need a destination in mind. After all, if you don't know where you are going, you've already reduced your chances of actually getting there.

When I started my company, Crafter's Companion, I had a very specific vision in mind for it. There was already a crafting company in the UK that I felt my products could compete with. The company was turning over about £4 million per year and was supplying around 250 crafting shops. When I was drawing up my own plans I looked at them and thought, *Yep, that's where I want to be.* So I learned as much as I could about how they worked.

We caught up with them relatively quickly, in no small part as a result of that laser focus. And once we were close to them in terms of scale, I needed to find another, larger crafting company as a model for what we could be. Only this time, there was nothing in the UK that was performing at the scale I now had in mind. So I refocused on another business, based in the United States, which had a turnover of about £23 million.

Looking at businesses that have already achieved much of what you aim to do yourself can aid your vision in two ways: firstly, it is proof that success is possible, and secondly, it can provide clues as to what you need to put in place to get there.

Then there's number three. I meet lots of people who are passionate, and some who have a great vision of what they want to create. But without this third essential – *drive* – they tend to fall short of their dreams. Drive works like momentum: it builds when times are good, but can slow when times are tough, so it's important to be conscious of your drive at all times. Rather than seeing it as incidental, you need to feed and maintain it.

There we go. That's the short answer. As for the long answer, in the rest of this book I'm going to suggest ideas, tools and strategies to infuse passion, vision and drive into everything you do. But you don't need to set aside hours and hours. Yes, of course you can't start, run and grow a business in six minutes a week – but you can learn a valuable lesson in six minutes, which is why I've called this book *The Six-Minute Entrepreneur*. I need you to put aside just six minutes every week to discover a valuable lesson in business – which leaves you with the other 10,074 minutes to apply and test what you've learned.

You can of course gallop through all of my six-minute lessons in one go (it will take you about five hours), but

Sara Davies

I'd recommend that you don't. Just as I've spent a business lifetime learning these lessons, I'd suggest you tackle them in bite-sized pieces, too.

Welcome to *The Six-Minute Entrepreneur*. I hope you enjoy the journey.

How to Use This Book

It's been proven that as human beings we are at our most effective when we have a clear focus, when we can put 100 per cent of our energy into a particular task. I'll talk about 'focus' later in this book, but for now, just take my word for it: focus is a key principle of success.

Therefore I've designed this book to help you focus on specific tasks that will maximize your performance. Each lesson follows a simple structure:

- Each starts with a 'story': some are quite short, some a little longer, but none are any longer or shorter than they need to be.
- Each story ends with a short summary of the key messages – I call this the 'takeaway'. The takeaway is the executive summary of what

you've just read and the messages that I want you to focus on for the next seven days.

- And finally you will be set a 'task'. These tasks are designed to help you apply, test and reinforce your learning. They are a way of enacting a principle and experiencing the difference that it can make. The tasks are the most important part of this book – some you will find easy, others more challenging, but be warned: if you don't complete them then your chances of maximizing your potential will be seriously reduced.

I've laid the lessons out in a carefully considered order, which means that some of them build on lessons from earlier in the book, while others cover completely new subjects. Reading the lessons in order will ensure you get the maximum out of this book.

One final note: if, like me, you are quite impatient, then you may be tempted to race through each of the lessons. Don't. Instead, take your time, read (and re-read) the 'story', think about the 'takeaway' and work through the 'task'.

By staying focused, I guarantee that as the lessons, and the weeks, pass by, you will see and feel the results.

Lesson 1
The Pen

**It's not what they give you,
it's what you take.**

THE STORY

My mum and dad had always been in business and it had long been assumed that one day I'd take over the family firm – a painting and decorating shop.

I enjoyed working there in the holidays and at weekends, but I wanted to learn everything I could before going into business full time, so after finishing my A levels I started a four-year business degree. As with most such business courses, I spent three of the years studying and one year on a placement. The placement happened in the third year, which gave me a chance to apply some of the lessons I'd learned in the first two years, as well as giving me some practical experience that helped when I wrote my thesis in the final year.

As I had the family business to go to when I graduated, I wasn't that bothered about where my placement was, so while most of my coursemates headed to London for junior management roles, I was happy to stay more local.

As luck would have it, my then boyfriend Simon's mum found me a placement with a friend of a friend who was part of the boom in crafting that was kicking off in the mid-2000s. Glenda was an artist by trade and she had come up with some really lovely designs for rubber stamps and founded a business on the strength of them.

The placement offered half the money I'd get working in London, but it was closer to home, family and Simon, and at a passing glance the business seemed to be doing really well. It felt like a good opportunity. But within days of starting, I realized that all was far from what it seemed. The company was failing, big-time.

It was months – if not weeks – away from going under, with staff being paid using the director's credit cards. But I'd just spent two years learning how to run a business, and I'd spent my teenage years watching my dad run his, so I thought I'd give it a go and try to turn things around.

The Pen

It was still the summer break, so I figured that I could give it a couple of months and if all else failed, I could just head straight back to university in September and miss the placement year.

I was so eager to apply everything I had learned to date, but I stuck to the two fundamentals of any business plan: cut costs and increase sales. If I could do that, I might buy them some time, return them to profit and hopefully save the business.

To cut the costs we had to let some staff go, which is never easy. We looked at how every penny was being spent. And I mean every penny – even the photocopier that was costing 10p a sheet had to be cut back. We had to get a handle on the money going out.

At the same time, we needed to shift the stock. We also needed to know what was profitable and what was not – we needed a sales plan. I figured that the best way to sell stuff is to talk directly to customers, so I jumped in a car and visited every craft shop I could drive to . . . Every sale was a step in the right direction.

I worked flat out – after all, there was nothing to lose, and I absolutely love a challenge.

Things were starting to improve, and although we weren't out of the woods yet, after a particularly good sales day I asked Glenda whether she would pay me some commission on sales – it's how the industry worked and, what's more, she wasn't paying me a penny as salary. She said she'd think about it. It wasn't exactly what I wanted to hear; I knew times were tough for her but I was only asking for commission on actual sales, and I thought she would acknowledge the big difference I was making.

Although the commission didn't appear, I had the bit between my teeth and kept going anyway.

Slowly but surely, we were turning this failing business around. I kept a keen eye on the costs and worked every hour I could to sell, sell, sell. Summer turned into autumn, and by the end of my placement I'd covered thousands of miles, making countless pitches. It was clearly paying off, and by the time I was due to return for my final year at university, the company had been transformed. Sales were up, it was back into profit, and it was even recruiting new staff! On top of that, I had fallen in love with the industry and the passionate customers, and even had an idea for a product of my own . . . but more about that later.

So, I went to Glenda and said, 'I've really enjoyed working with you and would love to come back when I graduate – how about it?' Honestly, I thought she would be delighted. After all, I'd saved her business.

You can imagine my surprise when instead, she said, 'I

appreciate that you've worked hard for the business this last year, so if you wanted to keep working for us, I could give you some production work cutting rubber stamps.' To top it off, she let slip it would be minimum wage, but what did I think?

You've got to be shitting me, pet, was what I thought. But what I said managed to be a little more diplomatic.

It wasn't all bad, though. As a leaving gift she gave me a pen. You know those flashy Mont Blanc models you've seen in expensive jewellers' windows? Well, it wasn't one of them. It was one of those ones with the four nibs that you click down. The sort you use for your GCSE revision. To say I was a little bit pissed off is an understatement. But years later, I realized what my real leaving gift was. I had learned so much about people, about business, about crafting. All of this was worth so much that I would never swap those twelve months for a pen, no matter how fancy.

The Takeaway

Never measure the value of an experience by what you are given; it's what you take from the experience that is valuable. If you only focus on the salary you're paid or the benefits you receive, you'll probably go through life feeling hard done by. The one part of any job that is pretty much unlimited is the experience that you gain from doing it, and if you're willing to learn from every situation, you'll find yourself rewarded in ways that are far more significant than money alone. My advice here:

- Learn from every situation – good and bad.
- Appreciate (and value) the opportunities you have.
- Don't define the value of an experience by how other people reward you.
- Experience is priceless, even the difficult stuff.

The Task

Over the coming seven days, reflect on three business experiences that you have had. Two should be positive experiences and the remaining one something that you consider negative. For each of these experiences use the following structure to record your thoughts:

- Describe the experience. (100 words max.)
- Describe what you've learned from the experience. (100 words max.)
- What would/could you do differently next time? (100 words max.)

"

Sara says:

I've deliberately given you a maximum word count for your notes. This will help focus your thoughts and make the task more achievable and much easier to revisit and review in the future.

"

Lesson 2
The Big Idea

Would you wrap a Christmas present in newspaper?

THE STORY

During my placement year with Glenda's crafting company, I really did commit to shifting that stock, and doing so meant travelling the length and breadth of the country to visit crafting shows. It was long hours of hard work, but I also gained an insight into an industry I was rapidly becoming passionate about.

I met fantastic crafters at every show I attended, but time and again I was noticing a glaring gap in the market. These craft demonstrators were creating amazing greeting-cards – seriously, *stunning* cards – but then shoving them into standard envelopes that half the time weren't even the right size! Some of the more enterprising designers and demonstrators out there were trimming their cards to fit the envelopes, but no one was creating envelopes to fit the cards!

Would you wrap a special Christmas present in newspaper? Of course you wouldn't! But to me, it's effectively what these craft demonstrators were doing, and they were encouraging their customers to do so too.

The more shows I attended, the more convinced I became that there must be someone out there with the kit to make envelopes that were up to the standard of the lovely cards. But nobody was. How could this be? Was I really the first to have thought of it? Surely it would be a huge seller?

It just seemed like such an obvious opportunity: to provide something that could help these crafters create an envelope that was the perfect fit and as beautiful as the cards inside. If I could just find a solution to this problem, wouldn't I have a product of my own to take to all these craft fairs? And maybe even beyond? Perhaps even on TV?

This is what some people call their 'light-bulb moment', when you think you really are on to something. But I had to be *sure*. Because even if you know your industry pretty well, and even if you have those flutters in your tummy when you really think this might be *it*, you can't do anything about it unless you have something more concrete than that. Nobody wants a young woman demanding you stock her product because she's got a 'feeling'. Nobody wants to invest in turning her idea into reality when the only evidence it will succeed is 'in her gut'.

I was fizzing with excitement about my big idea but I needed to check that what I thought was right, really was right. Luckily for me, I had a ready stream of customers to chat to at these craft shows, so I continually sounded them out. Glenda's company stocked some boards with various grooves on them so you could score the folds for a selection of card sizes to make bespoke greeting-cards. And I was used to the mental gymnastics of imagining paper in a variety of sizes – even if it was on the somewhat larger scale of domestic wallpaper, sold by my dad's painting and decorating shop.

So, when I went to the shows, I would set myself little targets of how many of these card-making boards I could sell. I found it unbelievably satisfying to slide the tools across the card, folding it *just so*, and ending up with a crowd of onlookers enjoying how neat and easy the whole process looked.

Wait 'til you see what you could do next, I wanted to tell them. But didn't. I stayed curious. I kept asking questions. I was prepared to learn something new. And while it was clear that customers were thrilled with the various cards they could make, they started to ask, 'Do you have the right envelope for that card?', and even 'Now can you show me how you make an envelope for it?' In time, my research backed up what had just started out as an idea. There was nothing like this out there and people were interested in it . . . I had my Big Idea – now the real work would begin.

The Takeaway

You may think that you have a great idea, but before you invest your time and your energy into making it happen, you need to do your research. Be prepared to learn and be prepared to be disappointed. You may have a good idea, but it may not be your 'Big Idea'. Think about what your customers need and want before you embark on a potentially risky journey. Remember:

- Talk to your customers!
- Listen to your customers!
- The time you invest now will save you time and money later.

The Task

Over the coming seven days, talk to three customers: two existing customers and one potential customer. Ask them the following questions. (You will need to modify them depending on whether they are current or potential customers.)

- What is the main reason you choose to use us/buy from us?
- What elements of what we currently do could be improved?
- What new products or services could we introduce that you would be interested in buying/using?

Look at the responses and ask yourself . . .

- Does anything about the customers' answers surprise me?
- What have I learned that I didn't know before?
- What am I now going to do differently?

"
Sara says:

It's very easy to become wedded to an idea because you've already invested lots of time (and potentially money) getting to the stage you are at. I often see this with entrepreneurs in *Dragons' Den*. While it's great to be determined and driven by your own idea, if you don't do your research and listen to customer feedback you can end up pursuing a dream that nobody else is going to buy into.
"

Lesson 3
Ideas Are Valuable

Ideas don't work unless you do.

THE STORY

Big ideas are valuable, so you need to protect them. Never, ever underestimate their value, even when you're just starting out. After all, when Facebook first launched in 2004, everyone was asking how it could ever be monetized. And now it's worth around $250 billion. We may not all be Mark Zuckerberg, but you never know how valuable your idea might be . . . until someone else tries to poach it. There is no point in doing your research and hiring your team, then realizing that your idea – your greatest asset – is vulnerable to being stolen. Trust me, I very nearly learned this the hard way.

When I conceived the idea for the Enveloper, I knew

that I needed to protect it, which is why I immediately applied for a patent. At the time, I thought it would be an overwhelmingly complicated process, but it really isn't. It only costs about £500 to submit your initial basic idea, and when the patent office acknowledges receipt of your application, this is known as your filing date. The application doesn't have to be too detailed; you just submit your idea and fee. Then you have twelve months until what is called your priority date – the point at which you need to spend the real money on a formally written patent application. What's important is firstly to get that initial date nailed down so there's proof that you had the original idea, and secondly that you remember you've only got twelve months before the next step.

It's an exact science, so you need to do it right – and crucially, you need to make sure that you don't tell anyone else about your idea before you sign that patent paperwork! I've mentioned that I often talk to customers to understand their thoughts on potential new products, as do my team. But we never talk to trade contacts as ideas can get shared. Sometimes it's by accident, but sometimes it's intentional. Either way, it isn't worth the risk.

Once on *Dragons' Den* we had a product come in that I absolutely loved. Whenever I like the sound of a business, I ask as soon as possible if they have appropriate patents and copyrights in place – and under what descriptions and in which territories. This is important because once it's been on television that idea can be endlessly replicated, with any commercial advantage lost. To my delight, the entrepreneur said that it was patented, so I put in an offer.

Then, after the show, came my own business team's due diligence: the moment when my lawyers look at the nuts and bolts of the deal. Although the show does its own due diligence prior to the entrepreneurs coming into the Den, my business team runs its own checks to make sure everything they say when they're actually in there is true, so that we know my investment is protected.

To everyone's dismay, my patent lawyer came back and said that the protection on the patent had recently expired: they hadn't met their priority date. Nightmare! They had been protected for twelve months before having to produce that second payment for the full fee, but they hadn't kept an eye on the timings.

Their protection had lapsed, and now the idea was out there. I was so disappointed that I couldn't then go through with the investment – the value of the business was in the IP (intellectual property), and with that now exposed, the business would always have been vulnerable. The tragedy was that it was a great idea, but it was now dead in the water because of some lapsed paperwork.

A patent is just one form of guarding the uniqueness of your product. Even if you are working in an industry where your product cannot be patented, you can still be attentive to what your USP (unique selling point) is. For some you will need copyright, while for others it may be something like location that needs preserving. The key is to pinpoint what makes you special, and to protect it either informally or formally, making it integral rather than incidental to your business plan.

The Takeaway

You may have a business that is impossible to patent, but the principle of protecting your idea still holds true. Be careful who you share your ideas with – they may just be about to become your biggest competitor. Keep the following in mind:

- Ideas are precious, so don't give them away freely.
- Talk to your customers, not your competitors.
- Small differences can represent big advantages in business.

Sara Davies

The Task

Patents protect an original product, but this week I want you to think about what you believe makes your business different. Your USPs (unique selling points) can be many and varied, and often offer clues as to why your business is succeeding.

Few businesses succeed because of a single USP; instead, it's often a combination of several factors. Not knowing what makes your business stand out and be successful can be very costly. For example, there are lots of restaurants that believe their USP is the quality of their menu, but when they move premises they find they struggle or even fail. Why? Because they had undervalued another one of their main USPs: their location.

Write a list below of what you believe are your business's USPs:

Reflect on the above list and consider how you can both protect and maximize these USPs.

"

Sara says:

Identifying your USPs will both help you to protect them from competitors and enable you to promote them to your customers.

"

Lesson 4
Are You a Believer?

Before you can create feelings in other people, you have to feel them yourself.

THE STORY

When I have a business idea, I can run the financials just by scribbling a few notes on a paper napkin; I can tell if it's going to make money. But making money isn't enough of a reason for me to do something.

Even if something looks like it's going to be good business sense, I need something more than that to pursue an idea. I need to *believe* in it. Because before you can create feelings in other people – staff, investors, customers and beyond – you need to feel them yourself.

This is also something that I look out for in the Dragons' Den. I need to know that the entrepreneur believes in the idea they are pitching to me – or why would I invest? Of course the numbers need to add up, too, but if I feel my heart beat a little faster as they tell me the story behind the product, and see the passion in their eyes when they pitch me their ideas, then I'm halfway to a positive investment decision already.

One of my favourite investments on *Dragons' Den* came about because of the passion I could see radiating from the entrepreneur. She had studied the Amazon product algorithms and discovered that huge numbers of people had the same problem: their young children and babies were knocking and throwing their bowls off their highchairs. Food was getting wasted and crockery was getting broken. What they needed was a bowl that 'stuck' to the highchair table. So she developed a brand and a product called EasyTots.

She was so passionate about the brand, she genuinely believed that these products would change parents' lives at an already stressful time. When she spoke, I was utterly convinced, which made her absolutely irresistible as an investment. Not only has she been a great investable opportunity, but she remains one of my favourite people to work with.

What I saw in that entrepreneur was authenticity. It's something that is very important to me, perhaps because I have learned over time that I am pretty terrible at faking it. I really cannot disguise my feelings if I'm not keen on an idea or a product – I let it show. I'm a useless blagger: if I don't believe in something, I just can't sell it.

I don't think I've ever let this happen with any of my company's products, but it did happen with our IT systems, a part of the business that I am less familiar with. A while back we updated some IT processes, and I had to explain to the staff that we were going through the long, laborious process of documenting all of our standard operating procedures (SOPs) to underpin the process. But because I had failed to really understand the process myself – through a combination of busy-ness and lack of real interest – there was little to no buy-in from the staff when it came to actually doing the work required. They had cottoned on that *I* wasn't interested and they understandably figured why should *they* be? As far as they were concerned, I was just asking them to do more work rather than less.

After a while I realized that the slow uptake was my fault. I needed to really understand how this set-up worked and how it was going to change things for all of us. I needed to buy into it, really envisaging it for myself, so that I could sell it to them as a positive idea. People can smell insincerity a mile away, and no good comes from it.

The Takeaway

If you don't believe in something, how can you expect anyone else to believe in it, be that a client, an investor or a member of staff? In other words:

- To be authentic, you need to believe in your own words and actions.
- If you don't believe, why should anyone else?

The Task

Having strong beliefs can be incredibly powerful. Some of the world's most remarkable people have been powered by their unwavering beliefs. Find the time to read about people such as:

- Henry Ford
- Nelson Mandela
- David Attenborough
- Ranulph Fiennes
- Anita Roddick
- Audrey Hepburn

Then write a list of the top ten beliefs that are key to what makes you and your business tick.

Sara Davies

Lesson 5
The Phone Can Wait!

Be present in everything that you do.

THE STORY

In 2021 I was invited to be one of the contestants on *Strictly Come Dancing*. I love the show and had watched it since I was at university, so being on it was one of my longest-held dreams. I knew that taking part was going to cause some level of upheaval in my business – and private – life, but I just had to do it!

Unlike some of the other celebrities, who were able to put projects as performers on hold and focus solely on dancing for the course of the competition, I remained at the helm of Crafter's Companion during the show – but I had a plan. To fit it all in, I'd get up at 5 a.m. and meet my dancing partner, Aljaž, at a little dance studio near me, to be ready to rehearse at 6 a.m.

On the way to the studio I'd be in work mode; reading emails, sending voice notes and checking in with what needed doing, I'd generally set things up for that working day, knowing I'd be back in full business-working mode by just after 10 a.m., when rehearsals finished.

So, come 6 a.m., when rehearsals began, Aljaž had my full attention. We would rehearse non-stop for two hours solid, me learning new steps and routines for the forthcoming show with absolute focus. Then we'd have a little break – a chance to rest our legs and for me to have a quick cup of coffee. I always ended up checking my phone. I'd read a few emails and send a couple of speedy replies, and then it was back to the dance floor.

But after a couple of weeks Aljaž pointed out that after our break at 8 a.m., I simply wasn't learning the routines in the same way. That focus had gone, and I wasn't absorbing the information or learning new skills as fast as I had been first thing. Maybe I was a little tired?

Aljaž's frustration made me stop and think about why I was focused at 6 a.m. but not after my break at 8 a.m. I'd told myself that I could somehow split my brain in two, that I could have work thoughts buzzing around my mind while dancing and vice versa. But I realized that I couldn't have been more wrong. I wasn't 100-per-cent present, which affected my focus and my dancing.

At first I was mortified, but Aljaž reassured me that he knew I was doing my best – after all, most years he didn't start training until around mid-morning! But we had to find a solution or I would continue to give only 50 per cent of myself.

So, I stopped checking my phone on that 8 a.m. break – after all, what was I *really* going to achieve by sending a reply two hours earlier?

It was undeniably the right thing to do. Here I was on the show I had dreamed about for years, and I could have blown it because I couldn't change a habit!

The change in my dancing was monumental, while the change in my business life was barely discernible, because I had been so clear about where I was and when I'd return. What I learned was the importance of being completely focused on the task in hand. After all, no one wants just a slice of your attention.

The Takeaway

Being able to completely focus on a specific task is one of the most powerful business techniques you can develop – but it's also not the easiest, so you need to give yourself every chance if you want to pull it off. So, remember the following:

Sara Davies

- If you want to perform 100 per cent, you need to be present 100 per cent.
- Reduce (or better still remove) potential distractions.
- Set time aside for specific tasks.

The Task

- Choose a specific intensive task that you want to complete this week.
- Set a specific time when you will embark on the task.
- When doing that task, turn off your phone, do not check your emails and do not allow *anything* to distract you!

When you have completed the task, ask yourself:

- Did I find the task easier or more difficult?
- Did I struggle to remain focused?
- Did time pass faster or slower?
- Did I feel more productive or less?

Being able to completely focus and be 'in the moment' is a skill that needs time to develop, so this isn't just your task this week, it's something you can practise every week from now on!

"

Sara says:

100-per-cent focus is a technique employed by all world-class athletes and sportspeople; their ability to literally shut off the outside world is extraordinary. They don't hear the crowd, they're not aware of the scoreboard, and they're totally focused and in the moment. When was the last time you saw a Wimbledon champion checking their text messages between sets?

"

Lesson 6
Hurdles

Hurdles can break your stride, but they don't stop the race.

THE STORY

In business and in life, you will all have hurdles to overcome. During my placement year at university I had a 'Big Idea' that I called an Enveloper, and I believed it could be a huge seller to all those creators who were making beautiful cards and shoving them into the wrong-sized envelopes. I'd done my research and I thought I was on to a winner.

I'd started out trying to create a prototype with a bit of help from my dad. We'd spent ages in the garage, tinkering with different sizes of wood from his box of odds and ends, but we just couldn't get the set-up quite right.

So, we spoke to an engineering mate of his at the local joiner's about how we could make it better. And after much more trial and error, we came up with a folding-board with the grooves in the right places to make the perfect bespoke envelope. Nailed it! Or so I thought.

The trouble was, this MDF prototype worked, but it was expensive to make, at £2.30 per unit, and it was heavy, which would have cost a further fortune to ship. I could still sell one for £3.30, which would have been a £1 profit – not too shabby; but if I could find a way to make it in plastic, it would only cost me £1 to make, it would be lighter, and it would give me a £2.30 profit per unit. A no-brainer, right?

Not quite, because to make it in plastic I worked out I'd need £30,000 to set up the manufacturing process. I'd have to get a plastic mould made to pour the liquid plastic into, I'd have to hire machines and have them running to get the things made, and I'd have to get the products to and from wherever they were being manufactured.

As a 22-year-old still living at home, this simply wasn't an option. And even if it had been, borrowing that amount of money felt like way too much to take on for such a small operation. This was a hurdle, and a seemingly massive one. But there was no way I was giving up on my dream – so I would have to do things in stages.

The path I took was to go ahead with the slightly

clunky MDF Envelopers, but only until I could afford to start making them in plastic.

Yes, it was a huge reduction in profit to use MDF to start with. And these profits were further reduced by the fact that I was paying my sister five pence per unit to blow off the sawdust from each one before they were sent out to customers! But some profit was better than no profit, which is what I'd have been making if I'd just thrown in the towel. Little by little, the company bank balance crept up, and before too long I had the required £30,000 and could set up the plastic manufacturing.

I would never have got myself into a position where I could order my own plastic mould for the Enveloper if I had given up at that first hurdle, or even dithered and let someone else fill that gap in the market. And although I didn't know it at the time, my Enveloper would become the product upon which my entire business was to be based. When I had my next idea – for the Ultimate Pro – I was reminded about the importance of overcoming hurdles once again. That was a more complicated board that would allow users to fold card to make gift boxes, greeting-cards and all sorts. But you guessed it: it was going to cost more to manufacture than the company had. One hundred thousand pounds, in fact.

By then, I had learned to expect hurdles from time to

time, and that overcoming them is about looking at options and thinking of alternative ways to do things. We continued to sell Envelopers until we had £100,000 in the bank. And then we moved on to the Ultimate, leaving our MDF hurdles behind us.

The Takeaway

Hurdles can break your stride, but they don't stop your race. In business, as in life, you will face challenges along the way, but it's how you respond to these challenges that defines your success. To summarize:

- If you expect to face hurdles along the way, then they won't be a shock – and shock can be the biggest stumbling block of all.
- Take time to think around challenges – explore alternatives and be prepared to play the long game.

The Task

This week's task is a bit of a knotty one, so be prepared to spend a bit of time thinking! I promise you the time invested will be well spent.

Think about a problem – the hurdle – that has been holding your business back, and then answer the following questions honestly:

Sara Davies

- What is the problem?
- How long have you had the problem?
- Whose fault is the problem?
- Who do you blame for this problem?
- Why haven't you sorted out the problem yet?

Once you've answered these questions, consider how you feel. If you're anything like me, you probably won't feel great. These questions are typical of the questions that we often ask ourselves when we face a problem or hurdle. The biggest flaw with this set of questions is that they rarely, if ever, solve the original problem.

Now try thinking about the same problem or hurdle, but ask yourself the following questions instead. Take your time – you will probably need to think a little longer about your responses.

- What is it you want?
- How will you know when you have it?
- What have you done in the past that you succeeded in achieving?
- What resources do you have that can help you achieve what you want?
- What do you do next?

Reflect on how you feel. Do you now have a next step?

Asking this second set of questions takes you to a different place, focused more on next steps than past failures or problems. This is because this technique focuses on the outcome, not the problem. The more you use the second set of questions when faced with challenges or hurdles, the more successful you will become at overcoming them.

"

Sara says:

Soon you will find that asking yourself the 'right' questions becomes a habit – I promise you!

"

Lesson 7
Set Out for Success

Be clear on what success looks like, and you'll recognize it when it arrives.

THE STORY

When you set out on a new business, a new project or perhaps even a new hobby or personal goal, it is vitally important to be clear-sighted about what *you* define as the enterprise having been a success. This was a lesson that I knew instinctively for a long while, but it was my time on *Strictly* that gave me the best illustration.

When a runner undertakes a marathon, they might have a very specific time-goal in their head. For another runner, it might be a case of wanting to simply complete the course or reach a certain fundraising target. Similarly, when some people go into business they have a figure that they would like their company to be worth within a certain amount of time. For others, they want to be stocked in a particular shop that their mum always considered prestigious. Or it's simply about doing better than their last company did, or just the joy of making a living out of their passion.

In each of these instances, the project can only be deemed a success or a failure by the person who set their parameters for success. Sure, people might think you 'only' made it round the course in X hours, or your company is 'only' worth X amount, but if it's what you set out to accomplish – who cares! And if you're not clear at the beginning about what you hope to achieve, you can find yourself swayed by the assumptions and comments of others. 'Ooof, you must have been gutted with that time' or 'Never mind, sales might pick up next year' could cut to the quick if you haven't been clear with yourself from the outset.

When I was asked to take part in *Strictly Come Dancing* I was beside myself with excitement, but I was also clear-sighted about what I hoped to achieve. The show was bringing me to a bigger audience than I had ever had before and I knew on some level that it would be 'good for business'. But that was not my main motivation – I'm not a full-time television personality; I was busy with my 'real' job at the same time as doing the show. I knew from the outset that I wouldn't have as long to train as some of the others. So, sizing up my chances against the competition, I decided that victory for me would be making it to the halfway mark, and anything on top of that would be a bonus. For me, it was a matter of staying in the competition for as long as possible in order to get the most I possibly could from the experience itself. The dancing! The costumes! The magic!

So, when I finally left the competition, I was distraught, but not because I wasn't going to win – it was because the experience was over. Rose Ayling-Ellis won the trophy that year, and she deserved it by a country mile. I was thrilled for her and celebrated her amazing victory. I also knew that I'd held nothing back myself, and could not have got more out of the experience even if I'd been in her shoes. Every year, there are some contestants who get further in the show than I did, but who I'm sure don't get as much out of it. I didn't win, but I still felt like a success. And a huge part of that was because of the vision I'd had for the result I wanted.

Setting these parameters for success is also important in helping you to curb the temptation to compare yourself with others – there is no greater waste of time! I remember when I first had my kids, I would sometimes feel like a terrible failure as a parent when I hung out with mothers who had decided not to go back to work.

I supported their choices and wanted to hear all of their news, but I would sometimes come away feeling horrible about myself. I wish that back then I had had the insight to remind myself that the issue was not our different achievements but our different *goals*. It's like turning up to the parenting Olympics without checking which event you've been entered into, then not understanding why you keep losing! Nowadays, it helps that I surround myself with other busy career mums who are also aspiring to be fantastic parents. Focus on the goals, and the rest will feel so much easier.

The Takeaway

Success isn't always about winning and it certainly isn't just about the balance sheet, so make sure you come up with a way of measuring what *you* define as success and then work towards achieving it. Remember:

- Success is often personal rather than public, so don't be put off if other people don't understand what you've set out to achieve.
- When you achieve your measure of success, acknowledge and enjoy your achievement.

The Task

This week I want you to think about how you measure success, both personally and professionally:

- Write down what you would define as success both personally and professionally for the next three months, twelve months and five years.

The next three months:

_____

_____

The next twelve months:

_____

_____

The next five years:

_____

_____

- Compare your measures of success – do they change over time?
- Can you now use these measures to drive your actions?

Revisit your 'measures of success' regularly to see if they continue to feel right or need to be changed. Reflect on your short-term measures to see if you have achieved them.

"

Sara says:

How you define and measure success will almost certainly develop over time, but it's important that you're clear on what you define as success at any given moment. Don't get sidetracked by other people's definitions of success, because they are unlikely to keep you motivated and focused.

"

Lesson 8
Know What You Don't Know

Minds are like parachutes – they only work when they are open.

THE STORY

Nobody likes a know-it-all, but one of the biggest lessons I ever learned was the enormous value of knowing what I *didn't know*! That might sound a bit back to front for a business book, but bear with me . . .

A year or so after the success of the Enveloper, I had worked my way up from presenting at craft fairs and trade shows, and was appearing regularly on the shopping channels in the UK. All the numbers said I was doing a great job, with Envelopers and Ultimates flying out of the warehouse whenever I made an appearance. I was feeling good about my skills as a presenter – and about myself in general, if I'm honest.

It was time to take things to the next level, and after a bit of luck and a couple of strategic live demonstrations at key US craft shows, I got myself invited on to the Home Shopping Network. It was time to take America!

HSN, as it's called these days, is a massively big deal in the United States. It was established in 1982 and basically created the model for TV shopping as we know it today. The company turns over $3.6 billion per year and I admired their set-up enormously – not just as a businesswoman myself, but also as someone who *knew* that they could take our budding company to the next level.

So off I went to the USA. I knew it was going to be a big moment for me and my career, as by this point I was one of the biggest fish in the pond that was the fairly small UK crafting world, and I knew I was good. So, when I prepared myself to present, I imagined more of the same, but with a bigger audience out there watching. But oh my goodness – the degree to which I had underestimated the size of their operation was quite something.

It was only when I arrived in the studio that I took on board the challenge ahead of me. You know how steaks, cars and beds are all that much bigger in the States? Well it was like that, but with cameras and lights and screens – and something called an IFB . . .

I was so woefully underprepared that I was going to have to think on my feet. I managed to get someone to explain to me that IFB stood for interruptible fold-back and was an earpiece that allowed the presenter to hear the producer talking to them – and to the rest of the crew.

I had never used one before. It was confusing enough to hear someone else's voice while trying to speak coherent thoughts of my own out loud, but to top things off, about 90 per cent of what was coming in through the earpiece was actually for other people – directing cameras and so on. I wasn't just out of my comfort zone, I was perilously close to being out of my ability zone.

There was no way I could bail out of the slot, though. It had taken so much to get here, the only thing for it was to be open-minded about the process and do what I could in the six or seven minutes I had to dazzle the whole network, and of course the whole country. So I gave it my best shot – and the first five minutes were awful. I was well aware I was falling flat – reinforced by the fact that I could literally hear the producer in my ear telling me that it 'wasn't going well so far'. Then, mercifully, I got to a big reveal with the perfect bespoke envelope that I was making, and the numbers started to shift. I could see bar charts rising as the sales increased on the huge screens behind the cameras. And as that happened the producer's tone shifted too, encouraging me, and then – hallelujah! – saying they were now going to 'run long' on the item and keep me on air.

I had got away with it by the skin of my teeth. It was a huge rush, but it was definitely a case of more luck than judgement. I could have made the whole day so much simpler. I could have done my homework, researching exactly how the show was run and brushing up on the things I had no experience in. If I'd done this, I could even have fitted in more training and rehearsal – but I'd had no idea how much I didn't know.

So, make sure you always do your homework, and give yourself time to fill in any gaps in your knowledge or experience. It could be as random as trying out an earpiece, or something more predictable like reading up on the history and the key players of the company you are pitching to. And remember: it's not just about getting 'caught out' on the things you don't know, it's about going into that important meeting or presentation knowing that you have prepared as well as you possibly could, so that when you ask any questions while you're in there, they will be a sign of interest, not ignorance!

The Takeaway

Ignorance isn't bliss; in fact it can be devastating, particularly if it happens on a big stage in front of a room full of people who could change your life. To avoid its pitfalls:

- Make an active choice to seek out what you don't know.
- Develop a growth mindset and learn something new every day.
- Never assume; prepare meticulously.

The Task

This week's task is to plan a foreign holiday. You might wonder what this has to do with business, but planning for a holiday is a great way of honing your skills of preparedness! When planning, there are lots of details that need to be confirmed to make sure your holiday runs smoothly. Think about the following:

- destination
- departure location and terminal
- flight details – airline, time, luggage allowance
- airport transfers, car parking, car hire
- the time you must set off

- cost of flights
- where you'll eat
- hotel address
- type of hotel room

. . . and the list continues. It might seem that the arrangements are almost endless, but they're all essential if you want the holiday to go without a hitch. Think about your next business meeting or presentation in the same way: what do you need to do to make sure you're fully prepared?

"

Sara says:

There is a well-used expression in business: 'Fail to prepare and you're preparing to fail.' It's one that's worth repeating to yourself on a regular basis!

"

Lesson 9
Small Things Can Make a Big Difference

If you want to be confident, get a good hairdryer.

THE STORY

It's essential to give yourself every opportunity to perform at your highest level on the days that count the most. That seems obvious, doesn't it? So at this point you might be expecting me to reveal some classic nuggets of business wisdom about knowing your business inside out, having all your figures at your fingertips or honing your pitch to perfection. Yes, of course that's important, but I'm afraid that's not what I'm talking about here.

So what do I mean? I'm *actually* talking about setting

yourself up to be your absolute best on the big days – the ones that will really change your business, and possibly even your life – rather than expecting yourself to perform with robot-like precision day in day out.

Let's imagine that you've spent months, or even years, developing your product and you've managed to get an appointment with a buyer who could transform the future for you and your company. The meeting is at 8.30 a.m. in a city two hundred miles from home.

If you work out how much time and money you have already spent trying to create that opportunity, it's worth making one final investment to make sure this last step in the process doesn't let you down. If that means booking a hotel the night before, staying with friends close by or booking a train rather than driving, then that's the kind of 'self-investment' that makes good sense. It means you can focus on being the best you can be, not spend your time worrying about traffic.

Whatever you decide, it's the sort of 'self-investment' that will lead to an optimum performance from you in the one hour that counts the most. No one wants to look back and feel that they fluffed a presentation because their heart was still hammering after the anxiety of a closed motorway.

A word of warning, though: some people confuse 'self-investment' with 'treats', but the two are very different.

Sara Davies

Self-investment is about the effect on your future; it's investing in yourself to ensure you're at the top of your game when it's most important. Treats are about the *feeling* that something will give you – the thrill of a little reward. So don't get carried away with the 'self-gifting' instead and make sure that you remain clear-sighted about which is which.

For example, I applied this principle when I bought a Dyson hairdryer. It could easily look like a treat (and I'm sure that's what my husband Simon still thinks it is). But because it's a professional beast of a machine, this hairdryer means that I can do my own hair for a TV show or public appearance when there isn't a make-up artist provided to do it for me. And I don't mind doing it at all; it's actually quite relaxing! Yes, it was £300 (and yes, I still wince when I say that price aloud) but the results are so much better than they would be with any other model. It's worth it for the effect it has on my mornings, and therefore my TV performances, which are directly connected to the success of my business. Because I'm better prepared, I can do my job better.

A friend of mine keeps a set of pillows and a fan in the boot of his car. He knows that the sound of the fan and the support of a good pillow ensures he sleeps well. So, if the hotel pillows are rubbish and there's no fan, he goes down to his car and brings in his own. He's even been known to buy pillows and a fan at his destination if he's working abroad, because he knows that's what it takes for him to be in tip-top condition for business the next day and he considers it a good investment.

What helps each of us to perform at our very best will differ from person to person, but you can work out what you need by thinking about what makes you most anxious.

The Takeaway

Making sure that you perform at your best is essential if you want to get that competitive edge, so investing in things that enable you to perform well, rather than just in the business, can be money well spent. To conclude:

- The best investments are the ones that are effective, but not necessarily expensive.
- Sometimes it's just about ensuring the basics are in place.
- Always ask yourself, is it a treat or is it an investment?

Sara Davies

The Task

Your task this week is to notice the little things in your life that appear to be limiting your potential. Don't focus on anything too big, like deciding you need to move house to get a better home office, because that's probably not happening! Instead, consider the smaller things that might be holding you back – it could be as simple as buying a webcam for those conference calls so you can look better on-screen, or an insulated mug so that you can have a hot coffee before you go into a client's office, or a stack of A4 notepads so you can write notes and keep an up-to-date To Do list. When you decide what you need, order it, use it and appreciate the difference it makes!

> ## Sara says:
>
> **Yes, I am giving you permission to buy yourself a present! But remember, it's not just a gift for being good, it's something that will help you perform at your very best – it's an enabler. It's amazing how often we don't invest in the most important business asset: ourselves.**

Lesson 10
The Power of Mentors

Those who know and those who don't.

THE STORY

Having a mentor can be a powerful way to supercharge your development. But in order to get the best out of them, it's important to understand that there are two types of mentor: the ones who *know* they are mentoring you and the ones who *don't*!

One of my first mentors was Duncan Bannatyne. He started on *Dragons' Den* when I was a business student at university, and like me, he seemed like a regular person with an ambitious dream. He was also based in the North East back then, with big ideas and tonnes of aspiration – as well as the drive to match. But, crucially, he isn't full of fancy economic theories and incomprehensible corporate waffle. With the best will in the world – and it *is* a compliment! – he just never seemed that special. *If he can do it, so can I.*

So, I bought his autobiography, *Anyone Can Do It*, and devoured every page. Now, at the time, he had no idea he was mentoring me. I didn't even consciously know I was looking for mentorship when I was in bookshops seeking out everything he'd written and learning whatever I could from him. But his work and how he made me feel about myself had a huge effect on how I approached my own business, in both my attitude and my actions. It was the first time I realized that normal people can achieve really big things if they work hard at it.

The great thing about mentors like Duncan is that you don't have to ask their permission, you don't have to ask for their time and you don't really have any costs – apart from the price of a book! So Duncan can mentor you, too. And of course, so can I. After all, if you have a copy of this book in your hands right now, you've sought out my mentorship in some way, and I can promise you that I'm going to continue to do my very best for us both.

The other kind of mentor requires a little more work – but trust me, the returns are worth it. These are the mentors who *know* they are mentoring you. And the key to getting their wisdom is that you need to *ask them to mentor you.*

Most people don't want to butt in with unsolicited advice (well some people do, but let's face it they're rarely the people you're looking for advice from). But most people do love to be asked for advice; they usually take it as a compliment and enjoy helping someone.

So if you want someone to mentor you, you have to put yourself in a position of some vulnerability . . . and ask.

I have done this with TV presenter Fred Sirieix. My background is in shopping TV. I can demonstrate products while chatting to the viewers, all on live television. If you've ever seen the Jennifer Lawrence movie *Joy*, you'll know the drill. And without wishing to toot my own trumpet too much, I'm really good at it. On the other hand, Fred is very experienced in reality TV, which is a completely different skill. So, when I started working with him, I asked him straight out, 'Fred, if you see anything that I could do better, or if you have any advice, then I'd really appreciate it. I really respect what you do and I want to get better myself.'

Over the time we've worked together I've learned loads . . . sometimes it's just a little tip that will help me learn some lines, and sometimes he gives me positive feedback that makes me feel great and improves my confidence. Whatever it is, I treat Fred's advice as invaluable.

Sara Davies

One question that I often get asked is, 'How do you choose a mentor – what should you look for?' The answer is that you'll know when you know! Mentors are the people you naturally gravitate towards: the people who, when they speak, you listen; when they present, you watch. They are the ones who grab your attention without you feeling that you're being taught something. You're just interested in what they're saying and how they're doing things, so finding yourself paying attention is a natural response.

People often come to me and ask me to mentor them, but sadly I don't have the time to commit to it. But my dad, who is retired, has all the time in the world and enjoys mentoring a young lad. If you want someone who *knows* they're mentoring you, select someone who really has the time and capacity to commit to you. Otherwise, stick to their books or podcasts.

It's also important to remember that mentors can come from the most diverse backgrounds, and they certainly don't have to be presenting themselves as a mentor. Yes, they could be a business leader, but they might also be a parent, a friend, a sportsperson, a coach or anyone whose way of doing things is one you admire. Look at what I learned from Aljaž's insights into my distracted dancing after our 8 a.m. break – a perfect example.

Some mentors will share only one life lesson, passing

through maybe with a single phrase, a chance remark or a brief meeting – but they still contribute to your learning. Others will be almost permanent features in your life, people you might end up knowing for years. They're all valuable in different ways, and it's important to never stop seeking them out.

The Takeaway

Being mentored is a powerful way to accelerate your development, by taking advantage of other people's ideas and experience to broaden your skills. A good mentor can change your life, whether they're aware of it or not. Always bear in mind:

- Mentors come in all shapes and sizes.
- Sometimes you need to give a mentor permission to mentor you.
- Some mentors are with you for a brief period of time, while some will last a lifetime.

The Task

This week's task is in two parts:

Part 1
Seek out some advice from someone who doesn't know they're mentoring you. Depending on how much time you have, you could:

- read a new book about someone you're interested in or their autobiography – it hasn't got to be about a business person; it could be an athlete, artist or politician
- listen to a podcast on a topic that you're keen to know more about
- watch a TED talk
- attend a workshop or seminar

Part 2
Write down at least one top tip a week from a mentor and refer back to it when you're in need of a dose of inspiration.

"

Sara says:

Creating a network of mentors is like supercharging your development, and the great part is that you can get mentored for free if you know where to look.

"

Lesson 11
Trust Your Gut

Just because you haven't been taught it, doesn't mean you don't know it!

THE STORY

I imagine that some of you might have heard about imposter syndrome. It's that uncomfortable feeling that you shouldn't really be doing the job you are doing, as you aren't really qualified to do it. It can strike when you're halfway through a presentation, holding your own in a board meeting or even at Parents' Day at school . . . when you're the parent.

If this rings a bell, don't panic. There is a way through. Most of us have suffered from it, including me. Around ten years ago we had built the company to around a £30 million turnover, which in turn meant that we were having to fundamentally change the way we did business. It was going to have an impact on funding, training, recruitment, product development – the lot. I had never understood what a paradigm shift was until I came across one, but this was it: a moment where we really had to change our thinking about a lot of things.

It felt overwhelming. After all, this had been a company started from the bedroom of my student flat, staffed for years by family and friends, and now we were having to bring in so many new people and ideas. I believed that as I had no experience or 'qualifications' to run a company as large as ours was getting, I should hire someone who did.

We brought someone in who had run businesses on this scale plenty of times, and who came highly recommended. And as I had started to see myself as a bit of an imposter in my own company, I thought he was going to be the perfect solution. So I focused on product development, selling the product and being the face of the brand – and left running the business to him.

But after a few months I found myself cringing a little at some of the decisions he was making, as well as the way he was handling these decisions. In bigger businesses, 'playing politics' can fly under the radar, as there simply aren't enough hours in the day to know every employee really well. But when we were at our desks, we were used to being pretty much within shouting distance of all our colleagues, and we all knew where we stood. Suddenly that was changing.

A stranger had come into the mix and started game-playing – saying one thing to one person then another to someone else – and it wasn't working. My staff weren't used to that. They had been used to dealing with trust and openness but now they were coming to mistrust someone who was supposed to be in charge. Perhaps he thought he was being really dynamic. Perhaps it had worked a treat elsewhere. But it wasn't working for us, and I had to make a change. After two years we parted ways.

When I reflected on what had gone wrong, I realized that despite not having been taught how to run a £30 million business, I still had a gut feeling for what it should look like. What I was lacking was the confidence to see it through. I hadn't had any formal training or education on running a business since leaving university, which had been about eight years before by this point. Sometimes I was still working from my university text-books when dealing with certain business principles!

But I did have a clear vision for the business and while I needed something solid to back that up, I also needed to maintain control. I was the leader, I had to take the reins. So I invested in myself and focused on working with a leadership coach who helped me to understand my personality profile and taught me various theories and principles about how certain personality profiles worked or might work better. For so long I had made decisions on the grounds that 'I see the world this way', but now I could see that my methods were often well-established models and practices used by many other businesses. These business principles always seemed to back up my gut feelings, anyway: it turns out I was far from an imposter – in fact I had been on the right track all along without even knowing it.

Today I employ people who have skills I don't, and they bring so much value to the company. But I also recognize that sometimes in life you just know things without being taught them, and that's why I will always listen to my gut instincts, too. Experience *and* intuition – that's the magic combination.

The Takeaway

Even if you're new to a business, don't ignore your gut feelings. Listen to them, examine them and, when necessary, act on them. Keep in mind:

- Just because you haven't been taught it, doesn't mean you don't know it!
- Gut feelings are a mixture of experience and intuition – they can't be bought or taught.

- Back yourself: you are the real deal, not an imposter!

The Task

This week it's about getting in touch with your gut, allowing your intuition to speak and letting your unconscious mind be your guide. If that all sounds a bit esoteric, don't worry, it's not – I promise.

What I need you to do is set aside ten minutes to let your gut instinct answer the following questions. It's really important that you let your gut speak – don't shut it down, no matter how outlandish or unexpected its responses appear to be! The truth is that those thoughts and feelings exist inside you, and ignoring them doesn't destroy them, it just hides them, which is not the same thing.

OK, so here are the questions (remember, let your gut answer them honestly):

1. Are you driven by money, success or both?
2. Does your business excite you?
3. What one change should you make to your business?
4. If you could earn more money in a less stressful way, would you do it?

Reflect on your answers. Do any of them surprise you? Listen to what they're telling you, acknowledge them and then decide how to act on them. Do you need to change anything about the way you're working?

> ❝
>
> *Sara says:*
>
> **While I trust my gut, it's not the only thing I listen to, and I'm careful to dig into my feelings to make sure it's a decision that has some logic behind it. As you'll discover in some of the later lessons, ego can blindside your gut feelings!**
>
> ❞

Lesson 12
Never Write Off a Plodder!

**'Remind me who won?' said
the tortoise to the hare.**

THE STORY

When Crafter's Companion started out, we were processing about three orders a day. Yes, just three. We were using an old-school Sage software package to process them, my sister was blowing the sawdust off the MDF Envelopers with a hairdryer, and I had a mate's mum doing the packaging and despatching. If it all sounds a little bit improvised, it's because it was.

Around the time I started to have a physical product to sell, my old schoolmate Meera told me she was a bit worried about her mum, Kamala. She was from a very traditional Indian family, and having spent the last couple of decades looking after her husband and family, she was getting really low at home by herself now that the kids had flown the nest. 'Are there any odd jobs you could get her doing?' Meera asked me. I had just the thing, and before long Kamala was packing up those early MDF Envelopers for us.

As the business grew, so did the orders, and before long we were handling thirty orders a day. Not long after, we were processing even more. By this point I could see that Kamala was really starting to struggle, which meant the despatches were getting behind. But although things were starting to get tricky, she didn't change anything. The way she saw it, I had asked her to pack and despatch some parcels and that's what she was doing. To keep up, she was just working longer hours and getting increasingly overwhelmed.

In business talk, she was working 'harder but not smarter': continuing to do what she always had, never questioning what could be done to improve the system. She was becoming a plodder. And plodders can be dangerous for business. But whose fault was it? It was mine, because I hadn't appreciated that, even in such a tiny operation as ours, I was still her manager – and I hadn't been managing her. If the speed with which the company had grown was taking me by surprise, no wonder she was struggling to keep up. If even I hadn't noticed how much the processes needed to change, how could she possibly have done, especially given the fact she had never been formally employed before? She was loyal and dedicated, and she thought she just had to work ten times harder, over and over.

You need a good dollop of innovation, of people who ask 'Why?', in any company – the ones who are looking out for, and are open to, new ideas. But what I can see all these years later is that you're never going to unlock their curiosity if you don't give them *permission* to change the system for the better. You'll just end up with employees who become frustrated and resentful. I had to empower Kamala to find a way to work smarter. In this case, the solution was a completely new software tool for the despatch system, but she was never going to present that solution to me without my blessing.

My business was built on finding out what customers were lacking and offering them a solution. That's exactly what the Enveloper is and why it's a success. And I now do the same with my team. These days, I always say to them, 'Don't come to me with a problem, come to me with a problem *and* a solution.' This simple phrase lets staff know that change is not just possible, but that I *want* them going out to look for it. I'm always looking for ways to improve productivity, to get more done with fewer resources so that we can reinvest that time and money into new business. And if we're all looking for these solutions, encouraged to question rather than plod, then so much the better.

As for Kamala, you don't need to worry that she's still plodding along. Although she was our first-ever employee and it was the first job she'd had in her life, she ended up sitting on our board of directors, running our company bank accounts and working hand-in-hand with our CFO. She has recently retired, after eighteen very successful years in the business.

The Takeaway

Some people are natural plodders, happy to do what they've always done, but without support and encouragement they can create pinch points in a company. It's the job of the manager to help plodders adapt and grow. Remember:

- Plodders can be reluctant to change and at worst can become very inefficient.
- Creating a culture of 'How can we do things better?' can unlock the hidden potential in plodders.
- Managers need to support and encourage plodders to help them grow and change.

The Task

As a manager, helping a plodder reach their full potential can be a tricky task, but the rewards can be worth it.

Your task this week is to think about a 'plodder' that you know from business – it may be someone that works with you or someone you interact with in another company or organization.

Ask them if they can spare you ten minutes to talk to you about their job and what they enjoy most about it. Explain that you are trying to understand more about motivation and that they could help you. Ask them the following questions:

- What do you enjoy most about your job?
- What do you find the hardest part of your job?
- What skills do you need to be good at your job?
- What skills have you had to learn since starting the job?
- What, if any, new skills do you want to learn?
- Do you have a mid- or long-term career plan? If so, what is it?
- When confronted with change, do you:

  A. embrace it unreservedly?
  B. think about how you can adapt to it?
  C. avoid making any unnecessary changes?

Sara Davies

After the conversation, take some time to reflect on what the person has said and ask yourself the following questions:

- Do you have a better understanding of their relationship with their job?
- If the person doesn't have a clear vision for their future career, do you think this affects their ability to perform their current role?

Now list as many attributes that they bring to their work as you can, both positive and negative. Then reflect on ways in which you think they could be made more productive in their role, if supported.

> ❝
>
> *Sara says:*
>
> It's easy to miss the plodders – they are rarely as outspoken as others – but invest time in them and they can be as valuable as the louder 'live wires' in your business!
>
> ❞

Lesson 13
The Power of Empathy

Put yourself in their shoes.

THE STORY

Good communication is about connecting – whether it's with your team in-house, with your audience on TV or your customers in the wider public. There's been lots written about how to communicate, but I think the key is you need to have empathy: the ability to put yourself in someone else's shoes, to look at a situation from their perspective and try to imagine what they might be feeling.

When I stand in front of an audience of any size, I ask myself the question, 'What are they thinking?', followed by another, 'And what do I *want* them to think?' It's the first question that is the most important, because if you don't know what your starting point is with someone, you can't plot your route to what you want them to think. How can you come up with good ideas on how to convince someone if you don't know what they're already feeling? In short, it's very tricky. And this is why empathy is so crucial.

On the whole, when you meet someone, you tend to remember less about the specifics of what they said, but more about how they made you feel. When it comes to passionate politicians canvassing votes in campaign mode or that favourite primary-school teacher who made you feel confident enough to speak up in class, their empathy can be very persuasive – more persuasive than most of us even realize at the time!

Perhaps you have a favourite comedian. Can you remember the punchline of every single joke they told when you saw them perform stand-up? Or do you remember the feeling of sitting in the audience or on the sofa, helpless with laughter, looking at the person next to you and nodding in recognition at the daft story you both just heard? I've seen Peter Kay dozens of times and I can barely remember what any of the routines were about. But I know how he makes me feel – and part of it is that he makes me feel seen. He's a northerner, of course – but it's more than that. He's just a regular person, talking about regular stuff. He could be my uncle! The collective moment of connection – that's the sweet spot.

Sara Davies

People who are empathetic communicators are just so much more effective at their jobs. Vicky Gill is the legendary Head of Wardrobe at *Strictly Come Dancing*. Yes, her job is to sort out our costumes for the shows, but she does way more than that. She builds a relationship with each of us contestants, winning our trust so that we feel safe not just to appear on TV in those outfits but to dance in them, too. She treats each of us as an individual, not just 'another dancer'.

When I started on the show, Vicky reassured me that I'd always have a bit of ruched fabric over the part of my body that made me feel the most self-conscious – my tummy. It was a worry that she simply removed for me, week after week. I knew the whole dress would be spectacular, but with her having paid attention to my tummy area, I knew I'd feel secure, too. And somehow, as the weeks went by, and I felt listened to time and again, my confidence started to grow. By the time I was due to dance the tango, I was wearing a dress I'd never have dared to even look at in week one, and had no tummy worries at all. Did I wear it because Vicky had told me how I 'ought' to look? No, it was because she had spent time understanding where I was emotionally and met me there, before starting to shift the dial. It was quite a sleight of hand!

I consciously use empathy in my communications

every day. It isn't just about what you say, but how you listen and how you respond.

The Takeaway

Use empathy to understand how your audience is feeling. By putting yourself in their shoes and understanding their situation, you'll be able to positively change the way that people feel. You may not believe this, but before I need to 'perform', and whenever I get the chance, I'll sit out in the audience's seats to get an understanding of what they'll be able to see when I'm on-stage. I even did this on *Strictly Come Dancing*; it gave me a unique sense of how the room felt and helped me to really connect with the audience. I have learned that:

- Empathy will bring you closer to your customers, suppliers and staff.
- People will remember how you made them feel, more than the words you said.

The Task

This week's task is to practise your empathy skills as you talk with someone else. You can do this with a member of your family, a friend or someone you work with.

The conversation should be as relaxed as possible – maybe settle down over a tea or coffee – and it can be about anything. While you talk, do the following:

- Focus on the other person.
- Listen to what they say.
- Let the conversation flow – don't overplan your questions, just let one follow the other naturally.

After the conversation, reflect on what you learned and how you feel:

- Was it easy?
- Did you enjoy it?
- Did the other person enjoy it?
- Did you discover anything unexpected?
- Who did most of the talking?

❝

Sara says:

Empathy builds rapport, and rapport is what underpins great relationships. When having a conversation, consciously talk less and listen more – people love being heard and you'll discover so much more.

❞

Lesson 14
Helix

It's not personal, it's just business.

THE STORY

Building a business can be all-consuming, both mentally and emotionally. It isn't just about the sales or the store openings, but about the people. It's a time full of highs and lows, with moments when you feel enormously proud and others when you question whether it's worth it at all. On top of this, in our earliest days, many of us rely on the support (and man-hours!) of friends and family members. They're often chasing the dream alongside us.

Consequently, most of us entrepreneurs are fiercely protective of what we've created, and when our business is threatened we quite quickly switch to 'parent mode'; it can feel as if your own child is being attacked and you'll do anything to protect it. But is that the right thing to do?

Not long after the launch of the Enveloper, my business was growing rapidly. Profits were looking good and we were putting plans into action to launch our next product, the Ultimate Pro, as well as purchasing our own plastic-production machines. Around this time, I received a call out of the blue. It was Helix – yes, that company you might remember for making rulers, setsquares and many of the other bits and pieces we had in our pencil cases at school. They were interested in the Enveloper – very interested. And they wanted to meet me. So off I went, always keen to talk about my star product and my growing company.

The presentation went well, and I thought it looked like they would place a big order, but as the days and then weeks passed we heard nothing. In the end they weren't even returning calls or responding to emails. I was being well and truly blanked. How strange.

Months later, at one of the biggest UK craft fairs, I saw that the company was launching the 'Helix Craft Room'. It looked an awful lot like the Ultimate. It struck me that the packaging was pretty much the only thing that was keeping them apart. What a rip-off! To think I had taken that meeting in good faith! I was furious and went straight into 'parent mode': they were attacking my business; they may as well have been attacking my baby.

What did I do next? Take a step back and think rationally? Of course not. I responded emotionally. I was over a decade younger than I am now and far less experienced. I'd never felt stung like this before. I had copyrights in place for my products and I had believed that a company like Helix wouldn't just go ahead and copy us, especially after that meeting; they had looked me in the eye – and then did this!

So, I fired off a solicitor's letter and set the wheels in motion for a legal battle. At that time we had the cash to fight the battle, which is something I'm not sure Helix had anticipated. But what we were lacking was the experience in legal matters and an understanding of what it could do to the company even if we did win. It had the potential to put me out of business.

I was being led by my emotions, and once you let this happen, the only people who really win are the lawyers. I was twenty-three; I had no idea that by being the one to start legal proceedings I had put myself at risk of paying all of Helix's fees if we lost. I knew I had a good patent, but I was also unaware that they knew that too, and in changing a couple of details they had stayed *just different enough* from my product. The company also seemed to know that by bullying me with equally combative legal letters, I might lose my nerve.

Simon and I had only just got married and it should have been one of the happiest times of my life, but within a matter of weeks I was spending endless hours on the phone to lawyers, a privilege I was paying for by the minute – literally: I'd hear the little click on the phone denoting that the next block of fees was now coming my way. The worst of it was that I didn't really understand what was being said on the calls. One night Simon asked me what had been discussed and I just sat on the end of our bed sobbing. 'I don't know,' I confessed. To which he replied, 'What do you mean you don't know? We just spent twenty grand on it today!'

In the end, we went into mediation and Helix stopped selling their product as it was. It can't have done that well anyway, as by the end of the year I saw it being sold in bargain bins around the country. It felt good, but oh, what it had cost to get there.

Years later I met someone who had worked at Helix, and they were taken aback by how personally I'd taken their 'Craft Room' product launch. They'd just seen a great product and decided to get into that market. Business is business; it was nothing personal. I can see that now – but back then I had taken a business decision to heart, seeing them as out to get me and out to destroy my 'baby'. I had let emotion cloud my judgement, and it could have cost us everything and more. From that point on, I have made sure not to react in the heat of the moment and to let emotions settle before I respond. I am mindful that company leaders are simply doing what's best for *their* business and their staff, and that it's not personal to me – this is the key to keeping my response in check.

The Takeaway

Don't let pride, ego or personality get in the way of doing what's right for the company. I'm not talking about being inhumane, about being disrespectful of others, but examining whether your response is business-related or more about your own ego or feelings. Above all, remember that you are not your product, and your product isn't you. So:

- Don't let your emotions cloud your business decisions.
- Do what's right for the business, not what's right for your pride.
- Be aware of your ego . . . it's a dangerous counsellor.

Sara Davies

The Task

This week I'd like you to be conscious of your feelings. All too often it's the ego, the emotion, the instant reaction that makes us act in a way that we may end up regretting. You might not have a big business decision this week, but in your life there will be something that provokes your emotions: the person that jumps the queue, the driver that cuts you up, or the friend or colleague that is late and keeps you waiting. Instead of reacting instantly, give yourself time to think about how you feel and then decide how you want to react. Removing some of the initial emotion often gives you the opportunity to make a better decision. Reflect on what your initial reaction was, and what it became with some thinking time, and notice anything you decided to do differently.

"

Sara says:

There is an old saying to 'sleep on it'. While you haven't got to go to bed before making a decision, do always give yourself time; pause before reacting. It allows the head to regain control over the heart.

"

Lesson 15
Know Your Audience

It's all about your audience, not you!

THE STORY

If you want to maximize your potential and build your business, then the simple fact is you need to know as much as possible about the people you're talking to, whether that's a room of five hundred people or a single person on a Teams call. I always take a genuine interest in the people I'm heading out to meet, and what makes them tick. Of course people like you to be well prepared for a meeting, but they also love to feel that they've been seen, heard and understood, as people.

Obviously, faced with an audience of five hundred, you can't get to know about each one of them individually, but you can get to know about the company they work for, the vision that they follow, the values that they hold and the reasons behind you being in front of them. For example, it may be that the company has had a change of management or has decided on a new strategic direction – understanding this can be critical if you are pitching a product or service, and could give you the opportunity to align what you offer with what they need. If it's a new contact we're about to talk to, then I'll look at the company's website, search for news articles about them, check out their LinkedIn and the pages of a few of their key staff. It's amazing what you can discover. Perhaps the person you're about to meet holds a sales role now but has a strong background in IT. Or you might spot that their head of human resources used to work for a company you already do business with. It's these nuggets of information that can become invaluable.

I'll also google individuals to try to find a photo of them. Meeting someone for the first time and greeting them by name is a powerful statement, and one which often blows people away. I'll also re-read emails and messages to see if I can pick up on subtle clues or hints that might steer me when putting together my content or agreeing an agenda.

When we were recruiting for a new CEO for Crafter's Companion, which is a role you'd imagine candidates

Know Your Audience

putting in a lot of prep to apply for, I could tell within minutes how much each of them knew about me and the history of the company. Needless to say, the ones that knew little or nothing about me or my company didn't fare so well! There is so much information about me out there, it's easy to find out how you might win me over or at least just show me that you care about what I think. How could I be dazzled by the candidates who had failed to take that into consideration?

It's a similar situation on *Dragons' Den*. All the Dragons are relatively public figures; you wouldn't have to do a huge amount of digging to know our likes and dislikes, learn about our businesses and discover some of our previous investments. Some entrepreneurs really do their homework before they come in, but sometimes it feels to me like some just haven't done that.

At the other end of the scale, I was recently blown away during interviews we conducted for a head of marketing. One particular guy was so well prepared, and this time he hadn't just done research on me or the company, but on the customers themselves. He had gone above and beyond by actually putting himself through the whole customer journey, to see what they might experience when they come across us for the first time – and then he delivered a presentation to us based on that experience.

91

He had – completely anonymously and independently – bought a product via our website in order to really get to know the customer experience, from finding the website for the very first time to the process of purchasing the item, noting how long it took to arrive and how it was packed, then receiving it and seeing what condition it was in. He also critiqued follow-up emails from us. And he hadn't just done this for our company; he'd done it for three competitors and compared us all!

He really knocked my socks off. No other candidate came close, because it wasn't just that he had looked up a load of stats about Crafter's Companion and its competitors, but that he had got himself into the mindset of our customers as well as those of a few of our rivals. He had proved to me that he was about more than just business jargon and surface-level facts and figures; he had taken his curiosity beyond the audience in the room on the day of his interview and extended it to the customers themselves.

Not only did I offer him the job, but by the end of the interview I felt like I was pitching *to him*, as he'd let slip that he was interviewing for roles elsewhere. He must have known how well he'd done by the time he left the building, and he deserved his success. Homework pays off, and it counts even more once school days are over.

The Takeaway

Learning about the company and its culture is important, but it can be even more powerful to find out about the individual people that you're dealing with. The more homework you do, the better prepared you are and the more likely it is that you'll be able to achieve the outcome you're hoping for. My advice is to:

- Research, research, research.
- Use the information you gather about a client or their company to nuance your message.

The Task

This week it's all about research. I'd like you to choose either a client or person that you currently deal with or a prospect you intend to target. Your task is to find out seven things that you don't already know about them.

You can do your research any way you like, but make sure you use more than one source . . . Wikipedia and ChatGPT don't know everything; in fact sometimes they're downright wrong. Check out their company website or find something the client has written themselves to see their communication style. LinkedIn can be a good source, and of course more personal social sites such as Facebook and X (formerly Twitter) can also turn up some nuggets. The trick is to look at multiple sources, not just one. That way, you're likely to get a more rounded and accurate sense of who they are.

Once you've done your research, consider how this additional information can be useful to you and how it can be used to shape any communication you have with the person.

66

Sara says:

I'll re-read emails, hunting for subtle clues or hints that might reveal something about the person who wrote them. Some people want detail, others prefer to discuss the 'big picture'. Look carefully and they often reveal which they prefer in the way they communicate with you. Get it wrong and one customer will feel light on information they consider essential, while another might feel bogged down with detail they feel is irrelevant. Shape your communication to suit your audience and you are on to a winner!

And finally, why not research yourself: find out what other people can discover about you – it can be quite fascinating!

99

Lesson 16
Shy Bairns Get Nowt

If you don't tell them, how can they know?

THE STORY

When I was young, my parents' decorating shop – which sold wallpaper, paint, tools, the lot – was a true independent. It was entirely owned by them, which meant that every single sale meant something to our family. It wasn't just that my dad might hit a target, or my mam might be in line for a promotion. Every sale meant more in the pot for our family, from dinners to dreams. Someone choosing to shop with us could be one step closer to us being able to go on the holiday we were saving for, or towards our Christmas presents, or towards reinvesting in the business or my mam and dad's next enterprise.

As a result, when my school friends would say that

their parents were letting them decorate their bedroom, or were getting a new kitchen or a new lick of paint in the hallway, I would be absolutely fuming when the next thing they told me was that they'd been down to B&Q or wherever. Why would you do that, I'd wonder, when we're right here, and it would make such a difference to our family?

It wasn't until I was older and had a chance to reflect that I realized I had no idea what half my friends' parents did for a living. Why would I? So why would my friends know about the shop – let alone how much it meant to us? It probably never occurred to them what a huge difference it would make to us if they shopped there.

Years later, when my parents took a back seat and my sister took over the shop, the first thing she did was to bring it online. Straight away you could order your paint and your paint samples from her – and by now they were doing colour-matching, so you could get your version of Farrow & Ball's Elephant's Breath ordered from your own home.

By now, I wasn't so shy. Whenever anyone I knew mentioned they were moving, decorating, even just touching things up, I was there like a shot with the website link and a quick 'You know you can order online from my sister now?'

What struck me was how much easier it was to say 'support my sister' than 'support me'. No one wants to feel as if they're nagging for a favour, but the fact is, if even you don't have the confidence to state how much it would mean to you, no one else will. More importantly, I realized that people very likely will use a business you're recommending if they truly understand how much it will help. So we have to keep telling them!

Recently, I remembered this while up on-stage at the Travel Counsellors Annual Conference. The business owners that I was speaking to were just that: small-business owners rather than employees of the big travel companies. They were self-employed micro-entrepreneurs and their financial security depended on how well they did.

Then and there I pointed out the impact I had made on my sister's business once I realized that people just *might not know* what a difference they could make with their choice of where to shop. It seemed revolutionary to people in the room – some of them confessed that their own family members weren't even booking holidays through them. But, like me all those years ago, how could they be annoyed when they hadn't yet made the situation clear? As is so often the case, at first it might feel uncomfortable, but if you're straightforward about it, it gets easier. And when you start to see results, it gets easier still. Shyness is not a business strategy, especially when you're starting out.

The Takeaway

Don't be shy about your business! Letting people know what you do makes it easy for them to choose you rather than go somewhere else. The more often you explain what you do, the easier it becomes and you'll be amazed at how interested many people will be. My top tips:

- Be proud of what you do.
- Share your message with passion and honesty.
- Explain the difference they can make to your business.

The Task

Have you ever heard of the 'elevator pitch' or the 'water-cooler conversation'? If not, then let me explain. Imagine that you have just the time it takes to grab a cup of water, or to travel a few floors in a lift, to explain to someone what you or your business does. Realistically it's going to be less than thirty seconds. In that thirty seconds you need to grab their attention and get them interested enough to ask you another question. It may sound easy, but if you've never tried to distil your entire business life into a couple of sentences then you may be surprised at how challenging it can be, unless you practise. But when you nail it, wow – it's such a great trick to have up your sleeve!

So, start by developing your own elevator pitch, and include something that would catch someone's attention – maybe a surprising fact, or something unique or unusual about you or your business. Leave your audience with the opportunity to ask another question and be ready to adapt your pitch to include something of specific importance to them.

Then test your pitch on friends and family, take feedback and be prepared to adapt. Confidently recommending yourself and your business to other people is a skill that deserves practice. Get comfortable acknowledging that what you do is great and that you are confident in yourself and your business's abilities.

66

Sara says:

I've heard some great elevator pitches – they might only take thirty seconds but they can lead to all sorts of unexpected and exciting opportunities.

99

Lesson 17
Know When to Take a Break

Rest days are as important as race days.

THE STORY

This week, we're taking a break. But I want to be clear: this is active, conscious rest. Not skiving.

We're not talking about the equivalent of those school days towards the end of term when the teacher would just wheel in the projector and let you watch a wholesome movie because they were just as frazzled as you were. This is me telling you to take a pause, because when you're training for something – whether it's your first 10k race or setting up your first business – the rest days are as important as the race days. And I'm ashamed to say that I didn't truly, viscerally believe this until relatively recently. In fact, it took going to the Arctic Circle to really appreciate it.

When you own your own business, you can fall into the trap of feeling that you never really have permission to be entirely 'off work'. For years I felt as if I couldn't do that; that I should always be available, no matter what. I could see with total clarity the importance of holiday and rest for my staff; if anything, I have had to come down quite hard on people for making themselves too available, sometimes at all hours. But always at the back of my mind was the fact that the buck stopped with me. How could that *not* mean being constantly available?

Then in 2024 I was asked to take part in a trek for Comic Relief in the Arctic Circle. It involved four of us over four days, out in the middle of nowhere, trekking through deep snow and freezing terrain – but worst of all, with no phone reception at all, let alone any visibility to see the phones or have warm enough hands to operate them! I was dreading it. No contact with my kids (though I knew they would be more than content with their dad and their grandparents the whole time). And no means of checking that things were going smoothly in the office.

Surprise, surprise, after about eighteen hours I discovered something: that I absolutely loved not having my phone. It was so liberating! There was nothing I could do to help anyone with anything while I was out there in the wilds of the Arctic, and not being able to be contacted by anyone was a freedom I hadn't known for years.

A lot of my time during those four days was spent on the enormous emotional and physical exertion of the trip itself. For several hours on the trot there wasn't much I was capable of thinking beyond 'Come on, you can do this, you've got to do this.' And when I wasn't thinking that, I was either saying it to, or hearing it from, the rest of the women on the trip. But at the same time, a part of my mind was able to detach itself from the constant sense of 'must check this, must check that' and I was free to reflect on bigger issues. And there is absolutely no doubt that when I returned, I felt all the better for it. A fresher perspective, a clearer sense of goals, and of course a sense of relief and achievement that we had accomplished our mission.

Obviously we can't all dart off to the Arctic when we need a bit of time to think. If that were the case, I know I'd be there at the start of every year! What I am talking about is finding your Inner Arctic, giving yourself permission to be truly 'out of office' for a bit. Can you find a day or a weekend when you could tell all the key people in your business that you are doing it, and then just put your phone aside in order to actively focus on rest and reflection? If you can combine it with some sort of physical exercise all the better. And if you still feel you need to be 'given permission' to do this . . .? Well, here I am, telling you that you have permission to be accountable to no one for a little while.

Even if you start with only a few hours at a time, heading out for a walk alone, or whatever is your chosen feel-good activity, will change your perspective. Don't let it slip to the bottom of your priorities – in fact, make it this week's top priority. Rest, reflect and then report back.

The Takeaway

We all need to take breaks, or else we start to become unproductive and will eventually burn out. But taking a break isn't just about physical location; wherever you go, you take your brain with you, so even paradise can be a noisy place if you don't get it to shut down. So, remember to get a proper break:

- Give yourself permission to switch off by booking out a specific time period.
- Notice if work thoughts begin to creep in, and if they do, try to consciously push them out of your brain.
- Bear in mind that the quality of a break is more important than its duration – little and often may work best.

The Task

Taking a break from all things work-related can be hard as we all take our 'business head' wherever we go, which is why physically occupying ourselves gives our brains time to switch off.

This week I'm going to give you a variety of tasks, and I'd like you to build up to a point where you're able to fit all of them into your diary.

Task 1

Buy some ear buds (in-ear headphones), download your favourite music and consciously go for a half-hour walk, ideally in a park or somewhere in nature. Allow yourself to be immersed in the process of walking and listening, not thinking. Repeat this three times per week.

Task 2

Make a lunch or dinner date with a friend or family member who is not involved in the day-to-day running of your business, and ask them about their life. Reconnecting on a regular basis with people outside of your business can really help put things into perspective and feel like a genuine break. Repeat every one or two weeks.

Task 3

Allow yourself to be entertained. Book a show or a concert, or just make time to watch a film at home. Turn off your phone, put down your iPad and immerse yourself in the moment. Do this once a month.

66

Sara says:

I find physical activity really helpful. Sometimes when I run, I choose to mull over work; other times I use it as an opportunity to completely switch off, clear my mind and focus on the scenery.

99

Lesson 18
Hunters and Farmers

You can't have a team full of strikers without a goalie.

THE STORY

Simon and I had only been married for a matter of months when we were confronted with the Helix fiasco, when it looked to me as though they had used my idea, and it took me a while before I could look back and see that I had learned way more from the experience than I had imagined at the time. Yes, there was the realization that I had to separate my own identity from that of my company, but I also learned how differently Simon and I behave in business – and where our individual talents lie.

During the Helix case, Crafter's Companion, although

still relatively small when compared with Helix, was continuing to grow at a cracking pace, and I was loving keeping up with the presenting, the ideas, the 'visions for the future' stuff. But I wasn't keeping an eye on the details, and as time ticked by and my attention was split in so many different ways, a few things started to slip. Back then, Simon didn't work for the company – it wasn't even something that we had discussed. He had a corporate job in a huge company based on the Continent and was used to working in businesses that size, with massive numbers of employees and budgets that would make your head spin. And he was working in Europe half the week, so I hardly saw him.

I knew he could make a massive difference to the company, but I would never have wanted him to give up his career to support mine. Also, he'd go from barely seeing me to being there every day; I was worried it would send him round the bend! But it was testament to his own self-knowledge that he quietly worked out what needed to be done, what savings could be made, and then presented me with more of a fait accompli than a proposal.

He explained that he had figured out that he could *run* the business while I *grew* the business; that we'd have very different roles, and that that was the best and only way to truly realize my dreams for Crafter's Companion.

He never put me in the position of having to ask for his help; he simply told me he would do it. So, one day he was Mr Shiny-shoes corporate guy, the next day he was working alongside his missus. And it worked.

It worked because I was the hunter and he was the farmer. It's something that I hadn't really thought about until then, but our skills and characters were quite different. While Simon is happy to tend to the business (to be the farmer), keeping it stable and profitable, I always want to go out hunting – build the business, find the next opportunity. This is why I love being on *Dragons' Den*.

The idea of having hunters and farmers is a bit like building a great football team: you can't have a team full of strikers with no goalie or defenders, and you can't build a team around having a great defence if you don't have any strikers to score any goals. But build a well-balanced team of hunters and farmers and you can have it all.

Simon and I worked out that rather than worrying about our differences, we could leverage them. I know he'd be pissed off if I started turning up to the meetings he's heading up, chipping in where I'm not best suited, and I know I'd be mortified if he started to muscle in on what I do, so we don't. We each know our strengths and we play to them.

The Takeaway

In business we need to be flexible, especially in the early days, making sure that we can adapt to whatever is thrown at us. But while being a Jack of all trades can be a bonus, we also need to make sure we're striking the right balance and playing to our natural strengths, be it farmer or hunter. Knowing which you are will help you focus on the jobs you are suited to, ensuring you maximize your effectiveness. To recap:

- Identify your natural role – it's where your strengths will usually sit.
- When building a team, strike the right balance between farmers and hunters.

The Task

This week's task is to understand whether you are naturally a hunter or a farmer. While most people will be capable of being a bit of both (life is rarely black and white), you'll tend to have a leaning towards one or the other.

Listed below are several pairs of statements about your preferred working style. In each case, tick either A or B:

I prefer . . .

Sara Davies

A. talking to new people and building rapport
B. maintaining long-term client relationships

A. helping people to discover new solutions
B. working with people to refine existing processes

A. getting a positive response from a follow-up call or email
B. receiving an enquiry from an existing customer

A. overcoming customer objections
B. presenting a solution that a customer accepts without question

A. hitting (or smashing!) targets
B. achieving steady growth

A. developing new products and services
B. ensuring existing solutions remain effective

A. brainstorming
B. scheduling and running regular reviews

Scoring your response

Add up the number of As and the number of Bs:

My A score was . . . . . . (max. 7 points)

The higher the score, the more strongly you prefer to hunt.

My B score was . . . . . . (max. 7 points)

The higher the score, the more strongly you prefer to farm.

> ## Sara says:
>
> **Knowing your natural style helps to maximize your effectiveness, but don't ignore the importance of both roles in building a business. This might mean working with or being part of a team that contains people with complementary skill sets.**

Lesson 19
Beware the Single-Product Business

Make it easy for customers to come back and buy, and they will.

THE STORY

As I've mentioned, when I started the business, there were existing crafting tools available for scoring and folding to create greeting-cards and boxes, but there was a gap in the market for creating bespoke envelopes. It was our Enveloper which filled that gap, delivering a solution to a problem that many existing craft customers hadn't realized they had. Customers could now make the right-size envelope for any card they created, and they loved it, buying the Enveloper in the tens of thousands and making it a huge success!

Beware the Single-Product Business

But . . . you only need one Enveloper. And the ones I was selling would never go out of fashion or wear out. It wouldn't need to be replaced in the way a sandwich, a bottle of foundation or even a football would do – and if these are the only type of products that you sell, that could in time become a problem when growing your business.

I knew that starting a company with one product was risky. While we were growing quickly, I knew that once everyone who needed an Enveloper had bought an Enveloper, they would stop buying – unless we could offer them something else! Yes, I wanted to take advantage of the gap in the market, but I also needed to develop follow-up products or my success would be short-lived. We needed to create products they needed on an ongoing basis, consumables such as card and paper, that they could purchase time and time again.

We started selling packs of paper that were pre-cut to size for the various different envelopes. Anyone can find a sheet of A4, but for larger cards you need larger paper and it wasn't readily available then. This allowed us to continue selling to our established customer base, cultivating the relationship and building the trust.

At the same time, we continued to work on a big follow-up product, which came in the shape of the Ultimate Pro, which could do everything – cards, envelopes and boxes. It was an opportunity to sell to customers who might have started elsewhere within our range, perhaps buying cards or paper, but once their confidence had been built, might buy the Ultimate Pro.

We had effectively maintained and cultivated our existing customers (farming) while still working on a new product to win new customers and expand the sales to our existing ones (hunting).

What is important to remember with this strategy is the need to respect the relationship with your customer – never take it for granted. The Ultimate Pro was a unique product, but if you're offering a follow-up product that already exists in the marketplace, you need to build in some kind of differentiation, either in terms of quality or in a unique feature that justifies the different price point, be it higher or lower. Never assume that just because it's 'you' that's offering it, they will leave an existing supplier.

Expanding our product line-up is how we continue to grow, all the time building the relationship and trust we have with our customers.

The Takeaway

Look at the products or services that you are offering your customers. If you only offer one product and it's something they only need to buy once, then you run the risk of never seeing your customers again. Instead:

- Make it easy for customers to come back by offering a range of products (and services).
- Differentiate yourself from the competition on price, quality or features.

The Task

This week's task starts with thinking about what you offer your customers (or potential customers). Take your time to list the products and services that you offer below:

In Lesson 16 we talked about how important it is to let people know what it is that you do, and now I want to build on that. When you have completed your list, think about whether all of your customers know about all of your existing products and services, and about how you can introduce these to customers who are not already buying them.

"

Sara says:

I have a friend who wrote training content for one client and produced video content for another. Both customers treated his business like a single-product business until he shared with them the full range of his services. Years later, both companies buy both products from him and he's successfully introduced some new ones to them as well, which has made his business even more valuable to his customers.

"

Lesson 20
Invest Your Time Wisely

**Where can your time make
the biggest difference?**

THE STORY

It's Monday morning, you turn on your computer and
start to tackle the overflowing inbox from the top down,
calling back the people who shout the loudest and keeping your eye on the biggest project that's in the works.
Isn't that something we've all done, even if we weren't
quite sure it was the most effective method? The truth is
that most people are responsive to what's coming at
them *now*, instead of assessing where their time can add
the biggest value. Don't worry if that sounds familiar;
it's the business culture that many of us are brought up
in, and it's a natural way to operate.

But time is a finite resource – it's the one thing you can't manufacture more of, so to maximize your potential you need to spend it wisely. The key to maximizing your potential is to understand your worth, so you can spend the resource of time more intelligently.

Let me give you an example. I know that I am the best person to present our products on-screen. My demonstrations make the biggest difference to sales – we have that data, and lots of it. So, working on that basis, it makes the most sense to prioritize my on-screen time. My biggest sales opportunity for most products is on HSN (the Home Shopping Network), the huge US-based network where we do a massive amount of business. In just four or five hours of on-screen time I can make a huge difference to our sales and profits.

But in the past I've found myself pulled in lots of different directions, squeezing in meetings during the run-up to a show or replying to urgent emails just as I'm about to go in front of the camera. But the numbers don't lie, and as a result of these distractions I wasn't as focused as I needed to be, and there would be times when I didn't maximize our sales.

Back when the business was still small, we only had about twelve staff and I saw a similar thing happen to my husband Simon. He was taking on more and more jobs on top of his existing role as CEO of Crafter's Companion. The buck literally stopped with him, so it was natural that if something else needed doing, he'd take it on – but that wasn't the solution. Yes, he *was* probably the best at a lot of what he was doing then – but trying to do everything was unsustainable. His time was finite and he wasn't spending it on the things that could make the biggest difference.

At that time I'd managed to persuade him that taking a couple of hours to teach someone else to do those 'other jobs' would be a good investment of his time, longer-term. He could liberate his diary to focus on the areas where he was most valuable. And it worked: he began to fill his diary with the jobs that made the biggest difference to the company.

I needed to do the same to maximize the opportunity with the HSN. Changing my working pattern, I had to focus my time on where I was most valuable and if that meant delegating or deferring tasks then that was what I needed to do.

All sounds pretty logical, doesn't it? But it's so much harder to let go than you think – particularly if you are a bit of a control freak.

Trust me, though, it does get easier the more you do it. What's helped me is to remember that a) you are empowering people around you, not merely dumping things on them that you cannot be bothered to do, and b) you will build your business much more quickly.

The Takeaway

Consciously and carefully evaluate where your time will be best spent to maximize its effectiveness. You may not get it right 100 per cent of the time, but you will still become more productive than ever before. To get the best results:

- Understand where you make the most difference.
- Maximize your time doing those things.
- Don't be afraid to say 'no' to projects if you don't have the time or don't see the value.
- Delegate tasks where possible.

The Task

To manage anything, you need first to measure it, so this week's task is to understand how you are spending your time. To do this accurately you will need to keep an accurate log of your time, dividing it into ten-minute chunks. It may seem like overkill to examine every ten minutes, but it's often the seemingly small distractions that can soak up your time and seriously affect your effectiveness.

Start your log from whenever you begin working – and that should include tea and comfort breaks, and travel time if you are out of the office visiting clients. Your timesheet should include a brief description of the task, and the exact amount of time spent on it. Give generic descriptions for the activities, for example proposal writing, prospecting, client meetings, invoicing, travel.

At the end of the day, review your timesheet and add up the total minutes – it should equal your full working day; if it doesn't then you've missed something off!

This part of the process is useful, but it's the second step that can be the most powerful. Once you have a breakdown of the time, give each activity a score between 1 and 5: items that score 5 are the most important, where you add most value, and the items that score 1 are the ones that are either not essential or could be completed by someone else.

This is not an exact science and some people are prone to analysis paralysis, spending longer on administering the timesheets than acting on the results! Try to avoid that trap.

The key part of this process is to get an understanding of where you are spending your time and whether that time is being spent most effectively. The results can be very revealing – but they still need to be acted on! Start to remove or delegate any 1s and 2s as quickly as possible, and focus your time on the 5s.

66

Sara says:

You may think you know where you make the biggest difference, but it's always worth checking with other people to see where *they* think your biggest skills lie. You might be surprised (and delighted) that something you didn't particularly value is seen as a real strength by others.

99

Lesson 21
Invest in Yourself

Don't spend money, invest money.

THE STORY

I don't like wasting money, but I also don't mind *spending* it when I know that something is a good investment. And over the years I have learned what a good investment looks like, which is why I firmly believe in making investments in oneself.

We've already talked about ways to make your working day *easier*, but the kind of investment we're talking about here involves ways to make yourself better at what you do. For some, this might feel indulgent, for others the idea of needing to be better might feel too self-critical. So think of it this way: if you'd invest the time, money and training in a staff member you really believed in and had high hopes for, then you should do the same for yourself. This is because it's all too easy to forget what *you* need to develop, even if you're being proactive and even generous with your own staff.

In my case one of the best investments I've ever made has been in presenter training. Over the years I've spent thousands. I've said yes to every course that the shopping channels – especially in the United States – have had to offer, and in addition I've invested in professional coaches who can help me develop. Presenting live on a shopping channel is not something it's easy to practise at home – after all, a big part of it is getting accustomed to all of the different screens, cameras and in-ear instructions, which is not a set-up that tends to be lying around at home for when I feel I need to polish my skills. So making sure that I have consciously invested into improving my presenting skills is my best method of staying at the very top of my game. Yes, it has cost me money, but yes, it has been worth it. You can see the results every time!

I have also made a considerable investment of my time reviewing countless hours of footage of myself presenting, as well as days watching other presenters, to really understand and home in on what technique is most successful. Could I possibly have made money in the time I spent doing this? Yes. But was the investment of spending all those hours and days on being the very best that I can be in the long term worth it? Absolutely.

I know that I'm the best presenter in shopping TV, and these days I have the numbers to prove it. What I am also sure of is that none of this has happened by accident: the harder I worked, and the more time and money I invested, the more accomplished I became. I can't get complacent, though, and I'm always looking for ways to improve.

Wherever I can, I will also take personal recommendations for ways in which I can invest in myself. For example, a few years ago I read *Strictly Come Dancing* judge Shirley Ballas's autobiography (another case of a great mentor), and in it she talks about working with a TV coach whose advice proved revolutionary for her. Within minutes I was googling the woman's name, scouring her LinkedIn page and approaching her to see if we could work together. We have, and I'm still successfully working in TV, as well as running my business . . .

So, next time you're about to spend money on yourself, separate the parts of the decision. Weigh up how it might *feel* to have that new thing, and consider the impact it might have on your performance. If it's something you personally want to own or experience – go ahead; we all need passions and rewards in our life! But don't then tell yourself it's 'for the business' or that you are 'making an investment'. However, if you can consider yourself as another invaluable cog in the wheel that is your company and its team, and you know that the business will make a return on it as a result, then it really is an investment.

The Takeaway

Even if you're at the top of your game, it's important to explore ways in which you can continue to improve. Remember, spending money is only wasting money if you don't get a return on that investment. Focus on the following:

- Stay hungry to learn.
- Don't just spend money *on* yourself, invest it *in* yourself.
- Investments can take time to mature, so don't look for an immediate return – if the investment is good, the returns will come eventually.

The Task

This week I'd like you to focus on investing in some self-development. The investment doesn't need to involve money, but it will require time.

Start by subscribing to two podcasts/blogs/vlogs that are new to you; you can choose whoever you want and on whatever subject you like, but I'd suggest that at least one of them is business-related. There are literally thousands of free resources, so your biggest challenge will be making the choice. At the end of the week you can carry on with both or swap one of them for a new one.

Whatever you choose to subscribe to, I'm confident that this extra input will trigger some fresh thoughts and broaden your perspective. Remember, this is an investment in you, because *you* are worth investing in.

> ❝
>
> *Sara says:*
>
> **If you don't already invest in yourself, start small by setting yourself the objective of making one 'self-investment' a month. Over time, as these self-investments begin to show returns, you will find it easier to commit to more and your returns will grow.**
>
> ❞

Lesson 22
Return on Opportunity

Returns come in many currencies.

THE STORY

We often talk about 'return on investment', but what do we mean? In simple terms, if I invest £1,000 in buying stock and then sell that stock for £1,200, my return on investment is £200, or 20 per cent. I've not included all the costs involved in making those sales, like wages, transportation, marketing etc., each of which will eat into my margin and give me my actual profit (which is the really important part!), but in the simplest sense this calculation has given me my 'return on investment'.

Calculating a return on investment in financial terms is usually pretty easy, but in business you can also be faced with investments that are not purely financial – these are what I often call 'opportunity investments'. I have already talked about the time that I invest in the entrepreneurs that I take on as a part of *Dragons' Den* and how that is repaid to me in terms far beyond the money of my original investment. What I'm talking about here is investments I enter into knowing full well that they won't make me money. In fact, by diverting my attention from my business, it might look at first glance as if they're costing me money. But the returns are about more than that.

I get lots of offers to speak at corporate events, make television appearances and write books on everything from making paper chains to making millions. All of these opportunities are wonderful, but to be honest if I took every single one, I would be away from the business so much that ultimately it would fail – the fees that I'm offered just wouldn't compensate the business for the difference I can make by being there on a day-to-day basis.

So, why do I accept any of these opportunities at all?

There are two reasons. Firstly, I know that my business can manage a certain number of days a year without me, as I have a great team and great systems in place that ensure it will continue to function. And secondly, these opportunity investments often give me a return that cannot be measured in simple monetary terms. In fact, this book is itself a great example of a 'return on opportunity'.

Putting together the content for this book has got me thinking, reflecting and analysing what I have learned over the years, and when I'm promoting my books or giving a talk, I often witness the light-bulb moment in people's eyes as they hear a nugget of advice that is just right for them.

This re-energizes me in a way that money alone can never do. So, while writing this book isn't making me money at the same rate that spending an equal amount of time in my business might do, the return on opportunity still makes it a great investment.

The Takeaway

If you only invest on the basis of a measurable financial return, then you'll be missing out on a lot of potential opportunities. My advice is to bake some 'opportunity investments' into your business plan, but keep the number right: there should be enough to keep life interesting but not enough to harm your key financials. In short:

- Choose your opportunities carefully – you still need to keep the business running.
- The best 'opportunity investments' will help you grow, sometimes in unexpected ways!

The Task

This week's task is about exposing yourself to the opportunity to invest in something that almost certainly *will not* provide a return on financial investment, but which almost certainly *will* give you a new perspective on life and a sense of purpose and positivity to your business. Choose one of the following:

A. Find a local charity to which your skills or knowledge would be valuable and offer them some of your time and expertise for free.
B. Plan a yearly fundraiser for a charity.
C. Ask staff which charities and organizations they belong to, and ask them if your business could support them.

> **Sara says:**
>
> **Giving back feels good and returns much more than you put in!**

Lesson 23
How to Become a Time Magician

**Multi-tasking isn't multi-tasking –
it's just kidding yourself.**

THE STORY

It's trendy to talk about 'multi-tasking' as if it's a must-have skill that no entrepreneur can ever get anywhere without. Well, I'm sorry to say that I disagree.

What I think people are really talking about when they discuss multi-tasking is the ability to *switch focus* effectively. We've already talked in Lesson 5 about finding a way to give specific tasks your complete focus, and this, taking things up a notch, is about switching that focus from task to task in a considered and effective way. Not flitting about, but making conscious choices. Being able to do this – shifting from one important task to another, even if they use very different skill sets – is an essential skill that will help you maximize your effectiveness. For instance, I enjoy being able to switch from presenting a craft show live on TV to leaving the set and having a proper chat with my mam about plans for school pick-up and the weekend before I tie up some work bits then head home for quality time with my kids. *Boom, boom, boom* – one after the other, no messing in between.

But for this to work, you have to be *completely focused* on the task in hand at each and every point. As you know, this is where I struggled while trying to run a company while also training for *Strictly Come Dancing*. I wasted time doing unfocused training, writing unfocused emails and trying to regain focus between the two. If you can't focus effectively, not only will each task take longer but your performance will suffer too. Your work simply won't be of the quality that you have the ability to actually produce.

So my advice is not to even attempt life as a 'proud multi-tasker'. I'm not even sure they exist! Instead, become an expert at *changing your focus*. Being 100-per-cent focused creates the efficiency and time-liberation that multi-tasking claims to but never can.

For example, don't 'keep an eye on' emails at work

when you're not expecting anything specific or important. If it's unexpected *and* important, someone will find you before too long. I keep two screens in view at work: one with documents, brainstorming for pitches and proposals, and one for emails. Most of the time I can easily and quickly switch between them if I'm waiting for something specific to come in, or if I'm just having a bit of general admin time. But I have learned that if I'm working on something that needs a lot of focus – that requires imaginative thinking or total concentration on the detail – the email screen has to go off. I've tried it too many times before! Every time I see a new email flash up, my attention is diverted to deal with it, giving me that quick serotonin hit of 'having taken care of something'. But it's usually trivialities I'm taking care of, tasks which could be done faster or better later on, when they're all I'm focusing on. And any time I save on getting it done now is time lost as I shift my gaze away again and have to refocus on what I'm *meant* to be doing.

The trick is to know which is a task where your attention can be split and which isn't. I know that in the kitchen I can chop an onion while catching up with Simon at the end of the day, but that I can't weigh out all the ingredients for baking while taking a call. I'll just sound distant on the phone or have to reweigh the flour over again!

Work is no different. I can't have those emails pinging away while I attempt the 'big brain' stuff. But I can save them up and have a good catch-up while I'm having my hair and make-up done (provided I'm fully prepared for what I'm about to do on camera – remember what I said earlier, in Lesson 8, about my first appearance on HSN). This way I can find some time where I'd otherwise be chatting nonsense, staring into space or idly scrolling on social media. I know that once I'm out of the make-up chair, I can focus on the next thing, no longer fretting about unopened messages.

The Takeaway

I structure my day by earmarking specific times to deal with specific tasks, instead of trying to handle multiple tasks simultaneously all of the time. This increases my efficiency, as well as the quality of my work. My advice is:

- Multi-task the simple stuff; change focus for the big stuff.
- 100-per-cent focus makes you super-efficient.
- 100-per-cent focus enhances the quality of what you are doing.
- Being super-efficient liberates your time.

Sara Davies

The Task

Do you focus best on deep work in the mornings, before you get too weary? Or is the morning the time to do the small tasks you can shift back and forth on? Or do you find that it's when you're grabbing a sandwich at lunchtime, or taking the train to work, that you can really blitz through your emails?

This week I want you to plan tasks that will fit in with your energy levels, allowing you to focus on specific tasks at the times when you think you can deal with them most efficiently.

Follow this process for the entire week and see if you are more efficient. Summarize your thoughts on what you have discovered using the space below.

> **Sara says:**
>
> There can be a big difference between being busy and being productive. If you can be both at the same time then you can move mountains.

Lesson 24
What's Important Is None of Your Business

Assumptions about your team's home lives don't pay, but being flexible about them does.

THE STORY

I used to do business with a company that was run by a husband-and-wife team. He was the CEO and she worked part-time to fit around their childcare. To me, that sounded like a great set-up. But it used to frustrate me that the husband was never available to talk before 9.30 a.m. After a while I found out why. *He* was doing the school run.

I didn't understand why his wife couldn't do the school run, as surely she had more time, and there were business contacts (like me) who needed to speak to him first thing. Back then, in my pre-kids life, I thought of the school run as an 'admin' job, something to just get out of the way rather than an important part of the day. When we were younger, Simon and I were consumed by the business. It was all we did and all we talked about. We lived to work, rather than worked to live. It was inconceivable to me that other people were not living the same way. Surely it should have been a priority for this man to be available for customers earlier than 9.30 a.m.? Why wasn't it?

These days, I cringe at the attitude I had back then. Apart from the fact that I had mentally relegated his wife to the admin tasks, I can now see how little empathy I had for that man and his life. Taking the kids to school wasn't something that was *getting in the way* of the important parts of his day, it *was* an important part of his day; it was his choice, and it was a highlight for him. Being in the car with his children, chatting with his family, was something that he cherished, something that he had made an active choice to prioritize in order to be fully focused on the rest of the day. By doing the school run in the morning, he was able to stay at work as late as was needed in the evening. I had patronized him by thinking he couldn't be bothered to put in the time, but now it's clear that that wasn't the case at all. After all, his wife was always in early and it was she who finished early to do pick-up. They had worked out their priorities and found a solution that met not just their practical needs but their emotional and family needs as well.

Years later, I know what it's like to have to juggle when you have kids. It is so important to be able to manage home and work, while making sure that you and your partner don't resort to feeling like shift workers who just pass each other as you make your way through the daily routine.

As a consequence of this realization, I made sure that we created a flexible approach to work across the entire company. This attitude differentiated us from other companies, and it paid dividends. I have both men and women working for me who could be earning more elsewhere but have chosen to work at our company because of the flexibility and quality of life we can offer.

Work is still a really enriching part of my life, but now it's not the only one. The catalyst for me was having children, but I recognize that it isn't just children or typical family set-ups that mean employees might have responsibilities outside of work. People care for extended family, or even friends, and have all sorts of reasons as to why this approach of empathetic flexibility is so important. We all want to work hard, but none of us should be expected to *only* work hard.

Here's something worth trying next time one of your

hard-working staff asks you for some flexible working hours on a Wednesday afternoon. Don't ask, 'Why do you need the time off?', which sounds confrontational and suspicious – after all, the person asking has already considered the time as important to them. If the business can work around them not being there, just say 'yes'.

There's another reason that I'm glad I've changed my perspective. When I first had children, I would tell a strange little lie, born only out of bravado. I never wanted anyone to know when I was going to a coffee morning at the nursery, taking one of the boys for their vaccinations or doing anything related to family rather than work during working hours. So, I would say I had a business meeting off-site.

I was so afraid that, because I'd had a baby, people would think I was slacking whenever I wasn't in the office, or that I had lost interest. It was madness, and in time I realized that not only was it not good for me, but I wasn't setting a good example, either. The truth is good people will recognize that being able to balance work and family life is important, and they will respect your honesty. As such, don't forget to give yourself permission for some flexibility for you and your family. You don't need to feel guilty about having a life beyond work, especially if you're role-modelling how to balance work and family to your team.

The Takeaway

We all have different priorities in life and it's important to respect other people's. Creating a flexible working environment can be extremely valuable to many employees. So, make a conscious effort to recognize people's other commitments and interests, and try to accommodate them whenever possible. Bear in mind:

- Many people place a high value on a flexible working environment.
- Flexibility is often an important contributor to loyalty.
- Say 'yes', not 'why?', if people ask for time off.

The Task

This week's task is about a shift of mindset and consequently a potential change in behaviour.

Book an hour out of your own diary this week. It could be a later start, an earlier finish or a proper lunch break. But whatever the reason, give yourself permission to take the time off and ringfence the slot in your diary so that it happens. Not only will this prove that you can step away for an hour, it will remind you that in life and in work you have choices.

"

Sara says:

Even if you're the boss, apply the same rules to yourself that you apply to your employees. Whether it's a school play, a dental appointment or a catch-up with friends or family, give yourself permission to take time out to do 'non-work' stuff, guilt-free.

"

Lesson 25
It's Good to Be the Newbie

Imagine every situation you're placed in is the first time you are seeing it . . . now what do you see?

THE STORY

I'm often asked why I took part in *Strictly* and the answer is always the same: 'Pretty simple really – I love the show!'

Seriously, it was my longest-held ambition to be a contestant. I was glued to it when I was growing up, and it's been a part of my run-up to Christmas for forever. I had talked about it for almost twenty years, and everyone from the office, the family and all my mates knew that if I were ever offered a chance to take part, I'd be grabbing it with both hands. How could I ever say no to the dancing, the dresses, the sense of community? So when I was invited, I had no hesitation in saying yes, even though I knew it would take a lot of sacrifice. People in the business had to work around me, my mam and dad had a huge amount on their plate helping out with the kids, and Simon had to step up and manage the family as well as taking on almost twice as much at work.

Entrepreneurs are addicted to challenge and opportunity, which means we're constantly stretching ourselves because we know that's what makes us grow. I am super-competitive at whatever I do, whether it's the school sports day or business, so once I got on the show I was going to do everything I could to stay in for as long as possible. It wasn't that I thought I would win, but more that I didn't want to let a single moment of it be wasted. I gave it my all, and I am sure that those around me weren't very surprised by that.

In the end, though, the real buzz didn't come from progressing in the competition but from working with a team of professionals who were all absolutely at the top of their game. The production crew, the wardrobe team, the make-up, the live musicians and of course my amazing dance partner Aljaž. You see, being in business can be a lonely place, even when you surround yourself with the best possible people. It can often feel like you are expected to have all the right answers, know everything that needs to be done and never show your vulnerability.

When I was on *Strictly* I was out of my comfort zone; I had so much to learn and had so many questions to ask. Being a newbie gave me permission to ask questions and get stuff wrong. The people around me kind of expected that I wouldn't know much, so they didn't find the 'stupid' questions stupid. In fact they enjoyed them: every time I asked for help they saw it as a signal that I was interested and keen to know more – and they were right. Suddenly I was getting valuable advice from *everyone* around me; being able to ask for it unselfconsciously and from so many different people was like adding rocket fuel to my learning. The tables had been turned and I was thriving on it.

I had been racked with guilt when I initially took on the challenge, seeing it as an indulgence. But now I recognize that it was one of the most positive learning experiences of my life. Not only had I learned about learning itself – about how I deal with taking on new information and skills – I had also learned about focus and how to manage my time when up against it in unexpected ways. And when I was eventually knocked out, I learned some big lessons about how to deal with adversity and disappointment. When I received the invitation to do *Strictly*, my mam told me that it was my 'time to shine'. Working on *Strictly* gave me a chance to become part of a brilliant team, not as a leader or manager but as a newbie. Knowing what it's like to be a newbie is a feeling that none of us should forget; after all, being a newbie is when we learn the most.

The Takeaway

Being a newbie can be wonderful, even if it's a little scary at times. Create situations where you have to operate outside your comfort zone and are relying on others to show you what to do. It doesn't have to be work- or business-related; instead, look for any situations that are unfamiliar. In short:

- Step out of your comfort zone.
- Give yourself permission to be the newbie.
- Watch, listen and learn from those around you.

The Task

This week I want you to become a newbie by trying something that you've never done before. At this point some of you may be feeling sick with worry while others won't be able to wait to get started. Whatever your emotion, don't worry – you're not alone. We all have different thresholds in terms of challenge and that can be accompanied by a multitude of emotions. A good way to become a newbie is to join an established club or group, like a sports team or running club. Maybe now is the time to take up a martial art or try your hand at learning to paint with watercolours. Whatever you choose, I want you to stick with it, embrace the sense of being a newbie, a beginner, and see how those feelings change as you become more established and more accomplished. For example, you may begin to feel less worried and more excited about the situation, you may begin to notice how the new environment begins to feel more familiar or it may be that you begin to feel more immersed and present. This task isn't going to be a five-minute wonder (trust me, I know) but what it will endow you with is a lifelong passion for learning.

66

Sara says:

Giving yourself permission to be vulnerable and ask the simple questions can be incredibly liberating when you spend the rest of your time 'being in charge'.

99

Lesson 26
There's a Time to Switch On and a Time to Switch Off

If you want productive staff, send them home.

THE STORY

When Covid hit, it was a huge shock for everyone in the company, and like most businesses we had to move fast, using what little time we had to come up with a plan. I have never felt the weight of responsibility as heavily on my shoulders as I did in those early days. Of course I wanted the business to survive, and I also wanted my staff to be OK – but it was hard to know what 'OK' meant in those early days. This was something no one had ever had to deal with before. There was no blueprint, no courses I could have taken, no mentor to reassure me that it would work out in the end.

During those early lockdown months, we all kept talking, supporting one another, and looking forward to how we would come out of it better than ever. Our distribution and warehousing operations were still active, so there was a lot of work on-site for many of the staff. Others were able to make the shift to working from home. And because so many of us were bringing up kids, home-schooling and dealing with caring responsibilities, managers kept their phones on 24/7 in order to respond to emails out of hours. We did what we needed to in once-in-a-lifetime circumstances. Back in 2020 none of us had childcare; everything merged into one – family and work, fun and necessity, even day and night! In those early days we had so many online meetings that it felt as if we all knew each other's lounges, partners and pets. There was even a point when I couldn't imagine being back in the boardroom without a cat or two wandering across key staff members' meeting notes!

Slowly, things began to return to normality. By 2022 we were functioning almost as we had been before the lockdowns. But what I hadn't anticipated was that it was going to be just as hard coming out of the pandemic as it had been going in. We knew we couldn't live like we had in lockdown for ever, but because of the nature of the country's – and the world's – return to 'normal' work, it was hard to know when we, too, should return to 'normal'. There had been such a definite, dramatic start to lockdown – the whole country was watching that broadcast. But readjusting as life started to take back its usual shape was gradual, incremental, different for us all. And for my team, a few things weren't changing back, though not in a positive way. Many of the managers were still responding to emails at all hours and had their phones switched on all the time. People were clearly thinking about work even when they weren't at work. There was no doubt that this was born of good intentions, especially as these were absolute stalwarts of the company, who had given so much during the hardest times. Their flexible attitude had been so helpful during the days of home-schooling, when so many of us were putting in a couple of hours at a desk once the children were in bed. But the kids were back at school and nursery now, so those team leaders had to stop being on call all the time!

We've always had some staff with jobs that require either late-night or early-morning communications, but it's clear that those are the staff dealing with the United States and China. They have breaks at other times of the working day to compensate for working those hours. But now we were in a situation where team leaders were – albeit unknowingly – creating a culture where emails were continuing on into the evening, encouraging people never to switch off. The world was no longer in lockdown and I needed the business to normalize.

I realized that it was going to take more than just a few words from me, because no one wanted to be the team member who was going to be the first to down tools at the end of the day! There were days when it almost felt like kicking-out time in the pub, trying to get everyone to go home – and to stay offline when they got there. Lines of communication had to be clarified and boundaries had to be redrawn. We were never going to return to life exactly as it had been before. We were used to a form of hybrid working now, and we knew each other in different ways – certain formalities had been erased in the heat of the crisis. I had to be very explicit with some of the managers that their good intentions were not always supporting company values. Once or twice I wondered if I would regret stressing the benefit of not working so much, but a couple of years on I can safely say that that has not been the case. Finally, we have found a path to having the best of both worlds.

The Takeaway

If your staff never switch off, the chances are they will 'burn out' and that's not good for them or the business. Being 'switched on' isn't necessarily just about being at work; people can be thinking about work to an unhealthy level even when they're home. To fix this:

- Lead by example: tell and show your staff that you take time to switch off.
- Avoid contacting staff when they shouldn't be working.
- Never assume staff are happy to work outside normal hours – always ask them whether they have the capacity to do so, and don't judge them if they don't.

The Task

Everyone has to switch off or else we burn out. One of the most powerful ways to do this is to give yourself permission and to signal to others that this is what you're doing. Your task this week will help you address both of these points. When your focus is away from work, whether that's during a lunch break or at the end of the day, I want you to set an email response to all incoming emails that explains that you are unavailable (or unable) to respond – you can do the same with your phone, directing all calls to voicemail. Choose a time period when these responses will be triggered; you can even choose who you would like the incoming messages to be redirected to.

Try using this response for a few days and see how you feel. You may want to change the timings or change the message, but don't give up on the idea of signalling to others when you are switching off.

> 66
>
> *Sara says:*
>
> **Being 'unavailable' will help you liberate time and can make you more valuable to others during the times you are available. Being unavailable isn't hiding, it's about focusing on other stuff instead!**
>
> 99

Lesson 27
Know Your Personal Brand

Know what makes you 'you' – and why.

THE STORY

When I was starting out with Crafter's Companion, working regularly on shopping TV and making a real success of it, I thought I knew myself. I thought I had a handle on how I came across and what my skills were. So, when I was doing my screen tests as part of the interview process for my role on *Dragons' Den*, I was surprised by the realization that I was feeling some internal pressure to be 'more Dragony'. Self-doubt had crept in.

It completely threw me. *More Dragony?* Up until

then, I had assumed I was there to be a bit different. In that moment, I was faced with a tricky decision. Would changing the way I presented myself help me get the job? Or should I stay true to myself and potentially lose out?

None of this had felt like such a big deal when I was broadcasting in the US or Germany. But now I was on home turf and potentially I'd be up there alongside genuine icons of both broadcasting and business. In that moment, I decided that when I was on TV, I had to be who I am and to own that decision, from how I spoke to how I looked. If it wasn't meant to be, I could make peace with it because I'd stayed true to myself. As you know, they liked what they saw and I landed the job.

I felt like I had the permission to sit in that chair, alongside the men in their Savile Row threads and Deborah Meaden in a bright, immaculately tailored power suit, while I was just wearing a purple spotty high-street dress. But that one thought still got into my head. Once we started filming, I convinced myself that deep down the producers wanted 'a bit more of a Dragon'. And I was absolutely overwhelmed by self-doubt. Was it OK for me to be me? And who even was I, now that I actually was a Dragon? My word, the ways I found to overthink it! Then I realized that in the past I had always had a product to hide behind; I wasn't selling 'me', I was selling an Enveloper, or a pen set, or a craft kit. Now, it was just me up there . . . *being me*. I was the product!

So I engaged a personal branding agency – not asking them to develop a brand for me, as I knew I didn't have a hope in hell of pretending to be anyone other than who I am, but asking me to help get *what my brand was* down on paper. They interviewed my family, friends and colleagues who had worked with me for years, and then presented me with thirty-odd pages titled 'This Is Who You Are'. Not 'This Is Who You *Should Be*', but who I *was*.

When I read that document, everything clicked for me, from how I speak to what colours I wear. I could see the qualities that others were seeing in me, and I could see that they were positive.

One of the main strands was 'Northern and proud', and even though I was, and I am, it meant so much to see it written down as part of my brand. It had always been my instinct to say things like 'me mam' instead of 'my mum', but the temptation had still been there to self-edit, to make myself seem 'more professional'. Now, I could say with confidence that it was part of my brand.

I was able to hire an agency to do the profile for me, and I have since advised so many people to go ahead and do something similar for themselves. We so often tend to assume that who we are and what people are seeing are the same, or that the things we feel we should change about ourselves aren't assets. But when you sit down and formalize your key traits, your way of doing things and what you stand for, then that's it: they become part of your brand. And once you know what that brand is, it becomes much simpler to stick to it, being guided by principles that you have formally set out for yourself.

The Takeaway

It's important to know who you are and how you want to be perceived, but it's equally important to be authentic and comfortable with what you project. Things to remember here are:

- It's vital to present a clear, consistent identity.
- Listen to other people to discover how you are perceived, and accept what they say is what they see (not necessarily what you wanted them to see).
- Don't try to be something that you are not – the cracks will quickly show!

The Task

This week's task is to understand your 'personal brand', how you want to be seen and what you want to project. You may already have a clear understanding of what you think you are, and that's great. The starting point is to write down seven points that *you* think describe your personal brand.

1.

2.

3.

4.

5.

6.

7.

The next part of the task involves other people. Ask a minimum of three people who know you in a work capacity to describe you in seven points. Explain to them that you want them to be as honest as they can and that it's part of a task you have been specifically asked to complete.

When you have all the feedback, compare it with your own perceptions. Are they aligned or different? Does anything surprise you? Is there anything missing that you feel is important? Is the way you are perceived by others the way you would like to be perceived?

Reflect on the feedback and think about how you can use this information to build your personal brand.

66

Sara says:

Knowing who you are and what you stand for is important. Being able to project that is equally important and will allow you to be authentic with yourself and your clients.

99

Lesson 28
Risky Business

Whose risk is it anyway?

THE STORY

I often hear people in business talking about 'risk and reward' but I wish I had known more about how to evaluate both when I was starting out. Because, as I discovered, if you get the balance wrong, it can end in disaster.

When I launched the Enveloper, I quickly understood that it was crucial to get the product on one of the shopping channels, preferably Ideal World. I had a contact there and was absolutely buzzing when she offered to make the Enveloper 'Pick of the Day' – the best possible introduction to the market!

I left their offices and literally did a little air-punch

that day. To top it off, they'd told me they'd need 8,000 units of the product to meet the demand forecast for that slot! It really was an absolutely cracking opening order.

Now, having just started out, I had no cash in the bank for the kind of costs involved to produce that many units. So, with the help of my dad, I persuaded local tradesmen to make them for me on forty-five-day terms, promising them that I had a huge order and they'd be paid as soon as I had received payment myself. After all, I assumed the sales were a dead cert because Ideal World was a big, reputable company. It's true that after that initial meeting I was struggling to get hold of my contact again. She simply never followed up with us. But I had a date for my broadcast, and she had told me in a formal meeting, on her business premises, that she wanted 8,000 units. So that was that. I took her at her word.

It took nearly everything we had to get those units made, including me paying my little sister five pence a unit to sit with a hairdryer and blow off the sawdust from each one before packing it up with an instruction sheet. Finally, the big day came and my dad said he'd take his van and drive them down to the Ideal World warehouse.

So I called the warehouse and told them we'd be delivering units for the show on 24 October, only to be asked for my purchase order number. Blithely I told them I didn't have one; they'd just need to get it off my contact internally.

'No, that's not how it works,' I was told. 'You provide the purchase order number, and then you book your delivery into the warehouse.'

Fair enough, I thought, still not that worried. Only this time, my contact did pick up – to tell me she'd changed her mind and it wasn't going to be a Pick of the Day any more – we'd get a number of brief appearances instead, which meant now they'd need only 1,500 units.

The floor felt as if it had dropped from beneath me. The difference between these being Pick of the Day or not was hours on air versus a few five-minute slots. And I had gone ahead and made the stock, as well as making some pretty big promises to the tradesmen who had been so generous with their terms for me. All I could think of was that cheque I had already written, ready to be cashed within forty-five days and counting. The sales on the 1,500 units wouldn't cover even a quarter of the unpaid invoice I was sitting on for the 8,000 units.

It's as clear as day when I look back on it now. I had been so excited about that order that I hadn't stopped to consider the risk involved – or whose risk it was. In this case, the risk–reward balance was far from in my favour: the reward was pretty even in that we would both benefit if the units sold. But if they didn't, then I was the one who would take the huge hit, not Ideal World.

In the end, I absolutely bossed my slot on-air, it was extended and we sold all 8,000 units. Ideal World even asked if perhaps we had a few extra units they might sell. But it's the understatement of the century to say that I learned a lot from that experience. For starters, it taught me that I needed to get a purchase order before I started manufacturing anything. Someone saying something in their office just isn't the same as someone giving you written confirmation.

These days, we are always very careful to share both risk and reward when we partner with people, especially when we are operating in markets where we're not specialists. We sometimes collaborate on ranges where there is an equal share of expertise on each side, and instead of us simply hiring someone for the project (thereby paying them and taking all of the risk ourselves), we set out a partnership structure where we are both bringing equal things. For example, we may make specialist products for the art markets, which are not our core focus. Our partner will devise the product and sell it specifically to their niche market, while we have the product made and take care of the logistics. We both share what our physical costs are, and neither is more exposed than the other to potential risk if things don't work out.

I love these sorts of relationships. It's about making sure you're not taking on all the risk and only getting part of the reward. After all, the latter is fine, but only if you've shared the risk first!

The Takeaway

In business you need to create situations where both parties have an interest in the risk *and* the reward. In simple terms, we both benefit from something going well, and we both suffer if it doesn't. Crucially, this keeps both parties interested. And when both parties are equally interested, the outcome isn't going to be down to luck alone. In essence:

- Assess the proportionality of the risk and reward.
- If there is no risk and no reward, there is no interest to make things happen.

The Task

It's important not to be frozen with fear; everything in life comes with some kind of risk, and we need to be able to rationalize what we consider acceptable.

You will, in your business journey, have already made decisions based on risk and reward, so for the first part of this task write down three situations where risk and reward played a significant part in your decision-making and assess whether you would make the same decisions now, if faced with the same scenarios.

1.

2.

3.

Next, ask yourself the following questions:

- What do you consider too big a risk to consider, regardless of the reward?
- What do you consider too small a reward, regardless of the risk?
- Has your threshold for risk moved up or down over time?

"

Sara says:

By managing risk, you can create a more balanced portfolio of projects that gives the business stability while keeping the door open for some more risky decisions.

"

Lesson 29
De-risking

Risk is a huge driver of behaviour. What would you try if there was no risk?

THE STORY

We've just seen how taking on risk can go wrong. To be honest, most of the time risk can seem too scary to bring up, so people tend to avoid it. But it's not all bad. If you address it correctly, it can be a potent driver of positive behaviour.

As you know by now, my husband Simon and I have quite different approaches to business – one of us is a natural 'farmer', the other a 'hunter'. So when, having joined the business, Simon saw an opportunity to draw some cash from the business to pay off our mortgage, we had quite different views. Simon suggested that by paying off the mortgage, at least we'd have a home if the business struggled, and we could live on very little and even get 'normal' jobs if we had to. I took a different view, and thought why worry about paying off the mortgage? The business was doing great, we were growing quickly and we could invest that money into growing even faster. If we did hit tougher times then I'd think of a way out of it – I trusted my business abilities.

To be honest, I really struggled with what I saw as a slightly negative attitude from Simon. Didn't he think we were going to succeed? Why settle a mortgage when one day we'd be buying a bigger house anyway? But after much debate we agreed, drew the cash, settled the mortgage and continued with the business.

About eight years later I was confronted with a similar situation. I received an offer to sell 25 per cent of the business. The offer would represent a significant amount of money, but again I didn't really feel we needed it – but again, Simon held a different view. He explained his logic to me. In the first situation, he'd wanted us to pay off the mortgage because the worry that we would lose the house if the business failed was stopping us from taking any risky – but potentially lucrative – opportunities. Paying off the mortgage would remove that risk. Now he was suggesting we sell the 25 per cent stake for a similar reason, only this time it would be enough money to secure our future: we could buy a forever home and our children's schooling would be taken care of. Effectively it took all of the risk out of our financial situation.

Being a hunter, I'm kind of familiar with risk – sometimes I even seek it out – but as a 'farmer' Simon wants to minimize it. So, what did we do? In short, even though I was hesitant to give up any of my control over the business, we sold the 25 per cent stake.

The cash did indeed secure our future, but for me the more important thing was that Simon stopped worrying. In addition to that, by de-risking our personal finances, I was now free to become more ambitious with the business.

Today I know that de-risking my family finances has given me more freedom, not less. It means I can take a calculated risk launching a new product that will cost me £100,000, because I know it wouldn't destroy the business if it failed.

This de-risking makes me more capable of making decisions that are right for the business. And because we are de-risked, Simon is more relaxed; and because he's more relaxed, he pushes me now and allows me to take more risks, which is what I need to thrive!

Sara Davies

The Takeaway

Risk can be addictive, but too much can be destructive. By de-risking in certain areas, you can take more risk in others, protecting you against failure while providing opportunities for growth. In other words:

- De-risking liberates your approach to growth.
- When risk is reduced, creativity can flourish.

The Task

This week's task is to play with the concept of risk. The task will work whether you are a natural 'farmer', 'hunter' or someone that sits pretty much in the middle.

Imagine that there is no risk, that whatever you decide to do in business will not damage it. In effect, whatever strategy you decide to follow would be risk-free. Now write down what strategy you would next pursue and reflect on what it could bring you if it succeeded.

When you have visualized what might be possible, it's time to build back in some risk. Think about what real risks might be present and factor them in.

The beauty of this task is that it forces you to think about risk and reward without exposing yourself to it in real life. It's a bit like fantasy football, and what it does is hone your skills of risk management and help you understand whether you might need to take more, or fewer, risks.

"

Sara says:

The task of imagining no risk can be quite a liberating process – you are literally giving yourself permission to dream! If you are risk-averse, you may find this quite challenging, but stick with it as you will learn a lot about where your fears lie.

"

Lesson 30

People Like to Know Where They Stand

Don't leave people wondering what side of the bed you got out of.

THE STORY

In one of my first jobs, my then boss tried to pay me a compliment which was wildly inappropriate but held a grain of truth. I was busy getting on with something when she said to me, 'Sara, I never need to worry about which day of the month it is with you.' How that boss was expressing herself was far from professional, but I chose to take it as a compliment. Whether in business, as a parent or as a friend, there is enormous value in being consistent. People respond to consistency – they know where they stand. They can predict how you are likely to respond if they need to make a decision without you. They can do their job without worrying that a nasty surprise might be around the corner.

We've all had that friendship where you wonder what side of the bed the person has got out of before you meet them. We all remember that feeling of trepidation, wondering if they'll show up, if they'll need cheering up or if it'll all be just fine and one of the good days. If that friend's erratic behaviour never changes, no matter how many chances you give them, it starts to wear thin.

Some bosses think that 'mood swings' or a sense of unpredictability is the way to keep their staff on their toes. I strongly disagree. That kind of behaviour is just an excuse for not being able to hold it together.

Think about the more junior levels in the business. Not only will they start to dread coming into work, unsure what 'mood' their boss will be in and unsure what type of performance will be required from day to day, but they will also learn by example that inconsistency is some sort of power move. That, in my book, is unacceptable.

Consistency *empowers* the people around you, whether you're acting as a manager, a friend or a parent. At work, you're letting them progress projects and make decisions safe in the knowledge of how you're likely to respond. Consistency also builds your leadership equity by showing you have a strong vision and clear direction. Even if people don't always agree with the decisions that you make, they will respect that you are consistent in your approach to both them and the task in hand.

But remember, consistency is about more than just being predictable. Predictability can imply flimsiness, a lack of imagination – but consistency is strength. It's about the courage of one's convictions, the confidence to act on them and the courtesy to embolden others to do the same.

The Takeaway

Your aim as a leader is to reach a point where someone can ask, 'What do you reckon Sara will think?' and your colleagues will be able to answer confidently, knowing exactly what you're likely to say. That is a real achievement.

Consistency is important because it:

- gives a framework for people to operate in
- removes your staff's fear of getting it wrong
- creates respect – whether people agree or disagree, they will all concede that you are consistent

The Task

Being consistent, by definition, requires an opportunity to demonstrate that you're being consistent, and that might not be something you can replicate on demand. So, this week's task is some self-reflection.

I want you to think of three times when you were faced with making a decision. They don't need to be big decisions, but they do need to be situations where a decision needed to be made.

Now reflect on the reasoning behind your final decision, and be honest with yourself: did you apply a consistent logic? How much emotion was involved? Would you change your decision if confronted with the same situation now?

In business, as in life, we all make the wrong decision from time to time – nobody is perfect – but being consistent is an important quality that empowers those around you, giving them a framework to operate within.

Sara says:

If you're tired, stressed at home or under pressure at work, shooting from the hip is not an option if you want the best from your staff, your team and yourself. Be disciplined with yourself whenever you feel your consistency is being compromised and take time to reset.

Lesson 31
You Can't Fit a Square Peg in a Round Hole

Square pegs in round holes fall out, eventually.

THE STORY

Hiring people is a delicate art, and it took me a while to understand what I was actually looking for in that crucial interview stage. It's not just about the skills – after all, these are evident on a well-presented CV. It's about the tone, the outlook, the personality. It's about looking for people who don't just have the experience but the disposition that will fit in with your company culture. I always say that we're a 'round-hole' company so I need to employ people who are round pegs . . . but I don't always get it right.

Years ago, I hired someone who wasn't a 'round peg'.

They had an outstanding CV and were clearly really good at what they did. No one else I had interviewed had even come close to their level of expertise and I really wanted them to come and bring it to us.

But there was also a part of me that was almost wincing even while I was interviewing them, as I could tell that they weren't 'our kind of person'. I tried to ignore the warning voice in my head, ploughing on and thinking *I can change that . . . we can roughen up some of those sharp corners . . . maybe make a hexagon . . . and get them to fit into our round-hole business.*

What a mistake.

Almost as soon as they started, I could see the problems emerging. They didn't fit in; they'd come from larger, more cut-throat, corporate environments. But I was so determined that we could make it work that I didn't even acknowledge the problems, pushing forwards and hoping that the situation would get better. But it didn't.

This person's colleagues weren't even thinking about their specific skills; all they could focus on was the mood that was being created in the office. This led to my staff starting to wonder whether I was as on-the-ball as they thought I was: *How come Sara hasn't noticed that there's a problem here?*, or even worse, *Why is Sara behaving as if this attitude is acceptable?* Over time, my team began to lose respect for me and that led to them starting to question my ability. In business terms, I was losing my leadership equity. I wasn't being consistent.

Leadership equity is the trust and respect you build up over time, earned as a result of weeks, months and years of good leadership. It is such a precious commodity, because it is perceived by others; it's not something you can simply buy in. This means you can't afford to lose it, because getting it back is incredibly difficult, and on occasion impossible.

Eventually I accepted that I had made a bad call and after agonizing for some time, I let the person go. It was difficult for all concerned because it wasn't their fault – they hadn't really done anything technically wrong; it was just a bad fit. The mistake lay with me believing that I could change them.

Every day that you have someone who isn't right in a key role, the rest of your staff are paying the price, dealing with a situation that shouldn't exist. I really care about the people I work with – they're everything to me – and I don't like employing any senior staff who don't feel the same way about the rest of the team. These days, I accept that a square peg is a square peg, no matter how dazzling their skill set might be. We're a round-hole company, and these days we stick to round pegs!

The Takeaway

You can almost certainly help people develop the skills that they need to do the job, but it's practically impossible to change their personality or their values. My top tips when adding to your team are:

- Consider the team chemistry – how would the new recruit gel with the existing team?
- Trust your gut – if it doesn't feel right, it probably isn't.
- If you are a 'round-hole' company, recruit round pegs!

The Task

Whether you're a new start-up with a single employee (you!) or a larger company with a burgeoning workforce, it's really important to know what you're looking for when you recruit.

This week I want you to write a list of ten personality traits that you feel everyone that works in your company should have. Remember these are traits not skills, so you can include qualities like honesty and loyalty, but not a specific qualification like the Professional Accountancy Qualification (PAQ) or whichever NVQ is listed, as these will be job-specific.

Sara Davies

1.

2.

3.

4.

5.

6.

7.

8.

9.

10.

When you have this list, put the traits in order, with No. 1 being the most important. Use this list as a reference when next faced with a recruitment decision.

"

Sara says:

Remember, if you are feeling someone is a square peg in a round hole, other people will probably be feeling it too. Don't ignore that feeling – act on it!

"

Lesson 32
Becoming a Leader

As a leader, love your people.

THE STORY

When you're starting out, you'll often be more focused on your product or service than on your people. In the early days, when your team might comprise barely more than you and a couple of others – and half the time those 'others' might be friends or family – you might be wondering who, exactly, you're leading? Your mate you did Brownies with and your dad? It can be tricky to behave like a leader if you don't actually feel like one.

It's understandably quite difficult to know what inter-personal or leadership skills you need when your day-to-day is all facing outwards as you make those first sales. But even if you're not implementing things in an overtly 'leadership' way at first, you do need to be thinking of yourself as a leader from day one. Unless you want to be a 'one-man band' for ever – which is fine if that's what you truly want – you'll have to learn to lead, or find yourself a leader who can do it for you.

So many of us set out in business because we're passionate about our product or our audience. But if you're going to grow, you need to start to channel that passion into your staff as well. Leadership is a skill as important as any other; it's simply one that can make you feel a little lonelier. But if you hire a team you really love and trust to take your business to new heights, then that in itself will give you the drive to lead.

When the pandemic arrived and lockdowns loomed, everyone was scared – worried about their jobs, their families and of course their health. I was feeling all of those things, too, but I was the leader: I knew that I had to set the tone for the company. If I showed any weakness, indecision or lack of confidence, it would have spread through the company like wildfire. It was time to lead.

What made that challenge more than worth it was the fact that I had no doubts about my love for my team. You can't just care about the business as an entity when a crisis like that hits, you have to see it as a collection of individuals. It's the same with your family: you'll find reserves of energy that you never believed you had when you need to protect them, to keep *them* going. It was this that gave me the energy needed to step forward and set out how we would head into lockdown.

The Takeaway

Leadership is not something everyone can do, and some people discover it in the most unexpected ways, but to be a leader you must love the people you are leading. If you don't care about them, then you can't lead them and they won't want to follow. Some golden rules:

- Leaders are always on duty.
- Leadership requires energy.
- Leaders must love and respect their people. This gives leaders energy!

The Task

Knowing how to pass on your passion and inspire your team is part of your role as a leader. This week I want you to:

A. List five things that you're passionate about in your work/business.

1.

2.

3.

4.

5.

B. List five things you're passionate about in your personal life – these might be hobbies, pastimes, friends, family, charities and good causes, etc.

1.

2.

3.

4.

5.

Consider how you would describe your personal passions if you were asked about them. Now use the same language and energy to describe your work/business passions.

Sara Davies

Did you find this task easy? Do you feel the same way when you talk about work as you do about your personal passions?

"

Sara says:

To lead a team, however big or small, your passion must be so obvious that it becomes infectious. This is why good salespeople can sell: their enthusiasm and passion shines through. And remember, love and passion go hand in hand – if you want to succeed, then love your team and be passionate about your business!

"

Lesson 33
Leader or Manager?

**'Management is doing things right;
leadership is doing the right things.'**

THE STORY

At first glance, leadership and management can seem like pretty much the same thing. I know it took me a while before I sat down and really thought about what sets them apart. But trust me, they are very different, and once you know how, it will change both the way that you work and the way that you hire. Because, after all, you need both roles filled in a properly functioning company.

When I first read author and management consultant Peter Drucker's definition, that 'Management is doing things right; leadership is doing the right things', I did a

187

double take. Although the wording is subtle, the impact is huge. To take it a step further, I define leaders as being about the *vision* – they are choosing the right path for the company. And I define managers as being about the *process* – they are making sure the company is keeping to that path, well equipped along the way. Very occasionally, there are people who can do both, but I know I'm not one of them! (A bit like how I'm a hunter, not a farmer.) I'm not a brilliant manager – there's too much process and not enough vision for me. So, it's managers who I really care about investing in, because I know I need people who are going to be all over the details. I'm an absolute magpie for those skills; it's a constant focus for me – to find strong managers.

If you're a leader, you need to make sure that you have processes in place to make things happen. If you don't, you'll find yourself struggling and frustrated when you can't move your strategy forward. If you're a manager, you need to ensure there is a direction of travel and a clear strategy in place, or you'll discover that you're managing the current situation well but are totally unprepared for what's around the corner.

An important thing to note is that these characteristics of leadership or management can manifest themselves at all levels throughout the business – staff members might not be in senior positions when they exhibit leadership characteristics. It might be evident simply in the clear-headed way they approach a task, or the way they influence their peers while the team is taking on a challenge.

One of my first members of staff started off without a team to lead – but she still behaved like a leader, influencing others in the business because her personality and experience gave her natural gravitas. I could spot from very early on that she needed a role in which she could use that ability, and all these years later she is excelling as head of our entire global customer service team. She is a born leader.

The Takeaway

Knowing whether you're a leader or a manager is crucial. In a small business you don't have the luxury of hiring staff to cover anything you can do yourself – you have to be capable of having more than one role in those early days. But it's important to start thinking early on about which one you naturally gravitate towards, and be conscious of which seems like the right fit for you at the right time. That way, when you can move on to hiring staff, you'll know what you're looking for. Always bear in mind:

- Leaders need managers to make sure their vision can be achieved.
- Managers need leaders to set the destination that they can work towards.

The Task

By now you should understand the benefits of being aware of how you spend your working time to ensure you are maximizing your efficiency – if not, revisit Lesson 23!

This week I want you to keep a timesheet to track your activity again, this time adding some extra detail that will tell you more about your role as a manager or a leader.

At the end of each day, review your timesheet and add either an 'L' for leader, an 'M' for manager, or even a 'D' for doer, next to each block of your time. (A doer is someone who cracks on and gets it done, and is rarely comfortable leading or managing a team. But sometimes you might figure out it's easier to do it yourself than delegate, so identifying the time you spend in all three roles is important.) You may find that there are times when you move between roles – for example, in a meeting you may shift from manager to leader as needed. That's fine – record both.

This process will help you identify the role that you spend most time in, as well as giving you an opportunity to think about the role in which you feel most comfortable.

There are no right or wrong answers here, but the results may surprise you – and it could give you a clue as to the role you need to recruit for next.

66

Sara says:

Not everyone is a natural leader; not everyone is a natural manager. And very, very few people can do both. Instead, focus on understanding which roles are needed and when, and put in place strategies to support this.

99

Lesson 34
Encouraging Innovation

**There is no such thing as a
bad idea . . . or is there?**

THE STORY

For a business to grow, thrive and survive it needs to innovate. But innovation isn't easy – so sometimes you need to get out there and look for it.

A few years ago at Crafter's Companion, we launched an innovation initiative, inviting every member of staff to put forward any new ideas that they had. We emailed the whole company and announced that ideas about new products could come from any area of the business, and that everyone was invited to present their innovations. We set up in the boardroom and whoever wanted to could come and pitch their idea to the senior management team. It was like a mini, company-specific *Dragons' Den* – I was so excited! Not just about doing things a bit differently, but also to hear about the new ideas and dream-products that our staff might want to share with us.

At first, there was a real buzz throughout the business, and we were all so encouraged by the response. There were people who really did get into it, and clearly put a lot into not just their presentations but the ideas that they were actually presenting. The senior managers and I sat through numerous presentations on a wide variety of submissions, before considering their merits and implementing those that we thought would work.

The whole thing went so well that we ran the same initiative again the following year. But this time we received a mixed response, in all sorts of ways. There was less buzz all round, fewer submissions from the team and, to be honest, some of the proposals were identical to the ones we had seen (and not implemented) the year before.

In short, it was a less successful exercise. But why?

There were two main reasons. The first was that we had not given participants proper feedback on the previous year's submissions. This was the reason that we had some re-submissions: if people hadn't been given an explanation for why their submission hadn't been implemented, they had assumed some sort of threshold had been reached on the number of ideas that could be carried forward, not that their idea had in itself been unworkable. And because they'd had no constructive feedback, they didn't try to develop their ideas. What a waste – and it was all our fault.

Secondly, some people simply hadn't enjoyed presenting their ideas the previous year, so despite having fantastic new ideas, they didn't want to go through the stress of it a second time. It had never occurred to me that there might have been serious innovators in the company who didn't have the confidence to stand up in front of senior management and take their shot. Again, this was a misstep on my part: because *I* both have vision for the company and enjoy presenting, I hadn't considered that others might feel differently about it.

What a waste of a talented workforce – and it was all down to me not thinking the process through. We should have made a clear distinction between the idea itself and the presentation of the idea. Those are two very different skills – not everyone with an innovation to share also wants to be a presenter. How could I have forgotten this when this exact division of skills is the magic that makes my working partnership with Simon so successful?

On the third year of running the scheme, we made

some changes. We made sure that everyone who submitted an idea had feedback, and that it was honest, constructive feedback. If it wasn't a great idea we would say so – but we'd also say why, so that next year's pitch could be better. And if it was a great idea but wouldn't work with our customers, we'd share that too, so that people didn't get disheartened by an unsuccessful idea that they'd rightly been proud of.

We also reduced the pressure from doing presentations, and instead started off discussing ideas in smaller groups, which could then be given feedback and refined without too much pressure. If the idea was good enough to progress to the senior management team, the working group could then decide who would present it. This took the pressure off individuals who might struggle with the spotlight, but let others shine if they felt up to it.

And it worked! Working in this new way, we got some amazing product ideas in all areas of the business and the feedback loop was much more robust. We acknowledged that even if younger staff members were really intimidated by face time with senior managers, they still had unfettered imaginations. They had been empowered to innovate throughout the company, and as a result we had some really off-the-wall product ideas that have now gone into production or will do so very soon.

Sara Davies

The Takeaway

Create opportunities that can unleash the potential of a talented workforce – after all, they're more invested in your business than anyone else (apart from you!). For example:

- Create an environment in which it's easy for staff to come up with ideas.
- Make a non-threatening environment for staff to 'present' their ideas.
- Always give constructive feedback, good or bad, and explain your reasoning.

The Task

Innovation can be incredibly valuable, and often it can come from the most unlikely sources.
This week I want you to encourage ideas and innovation within your business. The approach you decide to take will be affected by your particular situation – choose the one that suits you best from the following list.

A. Create an internal competition for employees to submit ideas – and follow the improved structure we developed!

B. Hold a brainstorming session with employees – you will need a facilitator to manage the time and collate the ideas. If you've never run or participated in a brainstorming session, there are plenty of top tips available on the internet.

C. Put an ideas box somewhere in the office and encourage staff to submit their suggestions. The ideas can be anonymous or they can include the creator's name. Think about ways of rewarding great ideas or submissions.

D. If your company is just starting out or has very few employees, then you can speak to a mentor about potential ideas you could implement or get together with other business people to exchange ideas and support each other.

> 66
>
> *Sara says:*
>
> **Gathering ideas and innovation isn't a one-off activity, it's an ongoing process. So be patient – but now is a good time to get started!**
>
> 99

Lesson 35

Keeping Your Tank Topped Up

Avoid the energy vampires and seek out the tank-fillers.

THE STORY

When I was in my twenties, before becoming a mam, I used to travel non-stop, and work non-stop while doing that travelling. I would use an entire flight to power through my inbox, work flat out for three days, take the red-eye home and then head straight into the office from the airport, ready to beast myself some more. But it wasn't long after having kids that I realized that this kind of schedule was unsustainable.

My body couldn't physically cope with it, but on top of that was the fact that kids are very emotionally taxing as well – not in a bad way, just in a demanding way! Until they came along, nothing outside of work ever really took an emotional toll on me. Once they arrived, however, my heartstrings were being played with day and night. Obviously I didn't (and couldn't!) ask them to take less out of me, so I had to work out what I *could* change and do that. Since then, I've made conscious decisions to boost my energy levels so they can stay high. It hasn't happened overnight, but it has been a shift throughout my thirties. I needed more energy, so I had to find ways to get more energy.

I've invested in the basics such as taking care of myself physically – training for fitness and eating well wherever I can, as well as being really disciplined about getting enough sleep, especially when I have to travel. Even so, there are times when I can feel that energy starting to ebb away. And if it can happen to someone as naturally up-and-at-'em as me, then it can happen to any of us.

There are two tips I have for maintaining and growing your energy levels. The first is to surround yourself with positive people. I'm not talking about avoiding people who are naturally more risk-averse than I am and who can easily be accused of being negative when confronted with new ideas – after all, caution isn't always negativity. I'm talking about actively choosing to work with posi-tive people who have a sparkling outlook on life, rather

199

than those who find 'positivity' in badmouthing others or who fail to go the extra mile when the situation demands it. You have to be aware of these energy vampires and manage your exposure to them, actively avoiding them if you've made a decision to do so.

The second tip is even easier. If you need to 'fill up your tank', then go and spend some time with customers. Doing this will never let you down – they are the ultimate reminder of why you're in the business you are. One of the ways I do this is to take a trip to a craft fair, where I love watching the crowds as they stroll between the different stands, groups of friends comparing things that have caught their eye and ideas they might try at home.

Dipping a toe back into where I started is always a huge boost. It reminds me that we are a business with a purpose, one that has customers whose lives are genuinely being made better by the time they spend with our products. I never want to forget that amid the busy-ness of running a business.

Sometimes I'll spend a day or a few hours in one of our stores. It is great to connect with the staff and customers in-store, and they always leave me feeling enriched, reminding me of the values our brand stands for and the impact it has. If I can't get out to one of the stores, I'll go online to one of our dedicated Facebook groups. These are specific safe spaces where like-minded people show their creations and encourage others. If someone admits they're having a bad day, the community will pick them up with suggestions of what to make, or sometimes just with cheering chat. It's a place where they all feel comfortable, because of their shared interest. Sometimes a new member will appear and nervously post the first greeting-card they've made, to be met with praise and a boost of confidence as others admire it. Seeing total strangers sharing their creations, congratulating each other over becoming a grandma or offering words of comfort if someone has suffered a loss, is a peerless reminder of why I do what I do.

The treasures made with our products are rarely about ego and more often about an expression of love, and that's a wonderful tonic on difficult days. All that from a business that began by solving the simple problem of creating perfectly-sized envelopes, which is hardly the height of glamour! So, whether you're in a business that provides a product or a service, nothing tops up your energy quite as much as seeing a customer whose day has been improved because of what you've delivered them. Make sure you never lose touch with the people that buy from you – they'll provide you with the energy to bounce out of bed in the morning, even if it's been a short night of sleep.

Sara Davies

The Takeaway

Energy is fluid, it can ebb and flow, so make sure that you keep yours topped up by surrounding yourself with positive people and avoiding energy vampires! Ways to do this include:

- surrounding yourself with positive people and positive energy as much as you can
- staying connected to your customers
- reminding yourself why you love what you do

The Task

This week I want you to talk to your customers. Ideally, I'd like you to do it face-to-face or by phone, but if that really isn't possible then email will do.

I want you to start the conversation by thanking them for their business, then explain that you appreciate them putting their trust in you (and your company) and that you want to ask them two questions. Then ask the following:

1. 'Why did you choose to buy from us?'
2. 'What do you like most about us?'

Hearing what your customers say about you and your company can be quite humbling, and you'll be amazed at what a difference you can be making to people's lives in ways that you may not always anticipate. This is the positive energy that I harvest as regularly as possible.

"

Sara says:

We all have friends or acquaintances that can be 'energy vampires' from time to time, and these can be as destructive as the ones we find in our business lives. So keep a check on the time you spend with your social 'energy vampires' or they might bleed you dry of the energy you need at work!

"

Lesson 36

Become a Recruitment Magpie

You often see what you need when you're not even looking.

THE STORY

I collect people's details and business cards wherever I go. This is partly because I'm very curious and always open to finding a perfect fit for a role and a person, but it's also because I often learn more about someone's suitability for a role when I talk to them outside of a formal interview situation. They're more relaxed, and subsequently they often reveal more. I then take their card in case the right opportunity comes up later on. Bingo!

In fact, some of the best recruits I've ever made for my business have turned out to be people I never even set out to recruit. I call it being a recruitment magpie – I'm always looking, even if I don't need anyone right now. We've already talked about how impossible it is to fit a square peg into a round hole, and developing your inner magpie can really help with this; it means that you might have the perfect round-peg-shaped recruit in your contacts already, and now you can save yourself having to 'make do' with someone who has the skills or expertise but perhaps not the best attitude.

Crucially, finding these gems is not an everyday experience. It's only every now and again that I'll come across an exceptional individual and think that they can really bring value to our workforce. But when I really believe in someone, I'll often recommend that they get into the business first, and then *they* can tell me how they might be of best use. Someone once said to me that 'you don't hire great people then tell them what to do', and it was great advice. I think it's a brilliant idea to bring someone who is visibly talented into the business and create an environment where they can succeed. That way, you'll not only get a job well done, but have the immense satisfaction of watching someone realize their full potential.

But be aware that not every recruit in your company can develop like this. Obviously, sometimes it's just a case of needing an admin recruit who's on the ball. And for that, recommendations are always a good idea – it's a hard skill to demonstrate in an interview, but no one ever regrets hiring an assistant who has been proven to make things run like clockwork while making it look effortless. Sometimes recruits grow out of admin roles, and if you've created an environment where people can really show what they're capable of, they will fly elsewhere in the company.

But when you're recruiting for roles higher up, you can make an approach to someone you've been keeping your eye on and see if they're interested. At Crafter's Companion, we have long had a culture where people aren't penalized for saying they don't understand something. I would rather they admit it and learn, than try to bullshit me – I can smell that a mile off and if someone does it, I won't trust them any more. Once trust is lost it is very hard to regain, especially if I recruited them because they were the right person with the right skills. But if you've made it clear that you'd rather questions were asked outright, then the situation can so often be avoided in the first place.

If you have created the right environment internally, you can teach an adept candidate any specific skills they might need once they're on staff. When people know that you trust their judgement, they can often surprise you with what they can achieve.

It may sound soppy, but you really do have to make

sure that you like someone when you hire them. I'm not talking about going for Sunday lunch with them every weekend, but having a basic sense that their core values are aligned not just with yours but the rest of the team's. And remember, it's far, far easier to do this if you get to know them outside of a specific interview role, while you're out and about, exercising your inner magpie.

The Takeaway

You can teach almost anybody almost anything they need to know to do the job, but if they don't have the right attitude, you're fighting a losing battle before you even start. It takes time to find the right people, so keep your eyes open for good candidates even when you don't have a job for them yet. My top tips would be:

- Recruit for attitude, not skills.
- Recruit people you like, because the feeling will almost certainly be mutual.
- Never stop looking for people, even when you don't think you need someone.

The Task

You may not need to recruit right now, but you can get ready for when you do. This week I'd like you to compile a wish list of potential future staff by writing down the attributes you know work well in your business. This will help you recognize them in someone you may meet in the future.

Knowing the 'must haves', the 'added bonuses' and the 'no-gos' will help you hone your inner 'recruitment magpie' and will enable you to spot a potential diamond when you see them.

66

Sara says:

If you already have a diamond in your team, pay close attention to what it is that makes their attitude and aptitude so special . . . and then go looking for it in others.

99

Lesson 37
Internal or External Mentoring?

**Some days you need a massage,
some days you need a sauna.**

THE STORY

I want to talk a little bit more about the mentoring
process. I mentioned the value of mentors earlier, and
that they tend to come in two types: the mentors that
know they are mentoring you and the mentors that
don't. But there are also two types of mentoring: internal
and external.

I'm an extrovert, and one of the main ways that this
manifests itself is that I like to talk things through. So,
when I'm working with a mentor, I do a lot of talking

(hard to imagine, I know!). Sometimes the mentor barely says a thing.

Thinking out loud helps me to align my thoughts, to make sense of a situation. It stops the thoughts from whirring around my head. I don't get shy about saying what I think or feel (yes, even harder to imagine . . .), so for me a good mentor is someone who's a good listener, who tends not to judge, even if they still challenge or nudge me as I wrestle with whatever problem I'm thrashing out. They don't give me the answers to my problems or preach at me, they don't dispense prescriptive wisdom from on high. It is more a case of them leading me through whatever is niggling me, often just asking the right question, which can flip the way that I am looking at things on its head.

This is external mentoring, and it feels like a mental massage. I'm working out the knots, feeling where the tension is and trying to get some more flexibility in my thinking. For me, the mentor is the masseuse.

Simon, my husband, is completely different. As he is much more of an introvert, he often self-mentors – he doesn't actually talk to a mentor in a formal capacity at all. He prefers not to express things he's not yet completely sure about, so he'll keep his cards very close to his chest, reflecting on a situation internally.

He's much better than me at having absolute focus regarding his problems, needing less external input. What he really needs is the space to think deeply – less of a massage from someone else to help with the knots, and more a case of fifteen minutes in a sauna with a bit of peace and quiet. He might look like he's sitting there doing very little, but just like someone in a sauna, his internal systems are whirring away, busy removing toxins ready to leave him feeling clearer all round before long.

Because we prefer our mentoring in different forms, Simon and I complement rather than antagonize each other whenever either of us has a problem – we both have huge respect for the other's way of doing things and reap the rewards of both approaches.

The Takeaway

You may already know which type of mentoring works best for you, or you may never have tried mentoring at all. Whichever the case, consciously try both internal and external mentoring to see which feels the most effective for you. As you do this, consider the following:

- People tend to prefer to either verbalize or internalize their thoughts.

Sara Davies

- The best external mentors often just listen and ask good questions.
- Internal mentoring can mean asking yourself for advice. You might not like the answer, but chances are it will be an honest one.

The Task

It's important to know whether you are more internally or externally oriented, as this will help you seek out the best mentors and understand your own behaviours. Ask yourself the questions below and respond as honestly as you can by allocating a total of five points for each one, using one of the following score combinations.

Scores:

A	B
5	**0**

If A is completely characteristic of what you would do and B is completely uncharacteristic.

A	B
4	**1**

If A is almost completely characteristic, but you might, on occasion, favour B.

Internal or External Mentoring?

A	B
3	**2**

If A is only slightly more characteristic than B.

A	B
2	**3**

If B is only slightly more characteristic than A.

A	B
1	**4**

If B is almost completely characteristic, but you might, on occasion, favour A.

A	B
0	**5**

If B is completely characteristic of what you would do and A is completely uncharacteristic.

Questions:

If someone else tries to tell me what they think I should do:

a) I would resist and try to use my own judgement.

b) I would welcome their opinions and consider their ideas.

A	B

Sara Davies

When I have completed a task successfully:
a) I don't need anyone to tell me that I have
done well.
b) I really appreciate other people confirming that
the task was done well.

A	B

If I have to make an important decision, I would much
prefer:
a) To work it out for myself, without outside
interference.
b) To find the best course of action by asking other
people what they think I should do.

A	B

Your scores:

Total A =   Total B =

There is a maximum of 15 points available.

If your A score is above 10, internal mentoring
will be your preferred style of mentoring.

If your B score is above 10, external mentoring
will be your preferred style of mentoring.

If both your A and B scores are below 10, you'll benefit from a mixture of both styles of mentoring.

> **Sara says:**
>
> **Even if you prefer one style of mentoring to the other, it's important to include a bit of both into your mix. Both are valuable!**

Lesson 38
Confidence

If you want people to sit up and listen, first sit back and listen.

THE STORY

That's right: say less. But I'm not talking about sitting back and doing nothing – rather, choose your moment.

When my company was a few years old and things were really starting to fly, I was invited on to the board of the CHA, the Craft & Hobby Association (now the Association for Creative Industries). We would meet about four times a year for the weekend, discussing pressing topics for the industry and taking the opportunity to do a bit of more general networking.

At first, I found sitting around that boardroom table hugely intimidating. I was years, if not decades, younger than most of the other people there. Despite the fact my company was doing so well, the fact that I had much less experience than the rest of the board was unavoidable. Consequently, in those first couple of meetings I was desperate to establish some credibility with the other members, and frequently found myself wondering how best to make an impact.

Then, after a year or so, I realized from watching the bigger names around the table that I didn't need to have an opinion on everything to make a valuable contribution. There was one gentleman on the board who seemed to think he did, but I can promise you after a few weekends of watching him butt in, talk over the top of people and make the same points that had been made perfectly clearly ten minutes earlier, I realized that quite the opposite was true.

This man was one of those people who, when he leaned in or raised a hand to speak, just made me want to roll my eyes. He wasted so much time repeating things, just to show that he agreed with others. Honestly, at times I found myself drifting off when he was holding court. Meanwhile, across the table from him was a chap who must have spoken a fifth as often, but I had ten times the amount of respect for him. More than once I observed the contrast between the men, before reflecting on why one commanded so much more weight within the room than the other. The answer was clear. The second guy said less, so what he did say counted for more. His approach of saying less conveyed a tangible sense of confidence. There was no sense of neediness; instead, when he did say something it sent the message that what he was saying was truly important.

What I also started to notice was that although he rarely spoke, he used very active body language when he wasn't speaking. He would lean in, pen to his lips, when something crucial was being discussed, or take careful notes when a detailed point was being made. Although he wasn't speaking, he was certainly part of the discussion.

I continue to use these tactics myself today: a combination of selective speaking and particular body language when at a boardroom table. And these days it's not just in the boardroom – I do it on-air as well. When I'm in the Den and an entrepreneur is pitching to us Dragons, I often hold back as long as possible if there is a product I'm really interested in. I don't need to rush in with my flattery and offers; I can show I'm listening in many ways, and I can be better prepared when I do speak if I have taken the time to truly listen and assess the situation. Then, when I say my piece, both myself and the others in the room know that I'll only say what really matters to me.

The Takeaway

It may feel counterintuitive at first, but it really is true that if you want to be heard in a meeting, say less. Stay fully engaged and show others that you are, then when you do choose your moment to speak, you'll command full attention. In other words:

- The fewer the words, the bigger the impact.
- Don't sell your ideas and opinions too cheap – save them for the important stuff.

The Task

Listening is a skill and the saying 'You have one mouth and two ears – use them in that ratio' is one that I often reflect on. This week I want you to consciously practise the skill of active listening in your next meeting or conference call. To help you be an active listener I want you to make notes, pay attention to other people's body language and remain engaged with everything that's being said. If there are multiple other people in the meeting, notice the role of the other listeners and consider who appears to have the most influence when they speak – you may be surprised at what you discover.

66

Sara says:

Listening is closely linked to empathy and rapport-building. Revisit Lesson 13 and review your outcomes from that task.

99

Lesson 39

What Happened to My Baby?

Businesses are like babies – they grow up.

THE STORY

You don't have to have had children to have been taken aback by how fast kids can grow. If anything, it's even more pronounced when you're an auntie or a godparent. One minute you're buying a cute teddy for a newborn, then the next time you see them they're a person who can tell you what their favourite food is and the name of their comfort blanket!

Businesses aren't quite as cute, and are hopefully a bit less prone to daytime naps – but the way they can catch you out by growing in the blink of an eye is alarmingly similar. And it's not just the growing – it's the changing, too. For me, this realization struck when one of my first-ever members of staff *left*. And at first I couldn't work out what had gone wrong.

Sophie had been with me almost from the start. We worked hard, and shared in lots of successes, and I thought she'd be with us for life, but as the business grew I noticed that she was becoming less happy, and eventually she threatened to leave.

Naturally, I wanted her to stay, so I tried everything to keep her. I changed a lot to try to accommodate her; I based decisions on what would be best for her; I did everything I could to recapture the mood of those early days. But nothing seemed to work – in fact, the situation seemed to be getting worse.

Then, when I was least expecting it, I had a moment of revelation. We weren't even discussing Sophie when one of my mentors explained that building a business is like having a baby and watching it grow up, and suddenly the penny dropped: Sophie had effectively joined one type of business, but now she was employed in another. It wasn't that she didn't want to work with us, she just didn't want to be in a company the size that we now were.

Like a newborn, your new business is helpless and completely reliant on you. This stage is hard work and you don't get much in return, but you find the energy to get through the sleepless nights and dirty nappies because the bond is strong and you love them unconditionally. You're working towards a future you've been dreaming of.

Then your business grows into a lovely cuddly toddler. Suddenly you get smiles and kisses! Yes, they still need your help but you're excited as their personality emerges and they start to venture further into the world.

School days see incredible learning as they develop new skills and interests, and in what seems like weeks they become a teenager – surly, grumpy and fighting for independence as they try to find their feet with you less able to watch their every move. You have tough times and occasional disagreements. Sometimes you even wonder what on earth you've created! You have to learn new ways of communicating, new strategies for coping, and from time to time it feels like they're pushing you to your very limits.

Then, in a flash, they are an adult – self-directed, independent and able to cope without you, even if they still need you really. You love them and they you, but their life is now their own. Now, your business – like your young adult – has its own identity and you can feel justifiably proud of what you have created.

Some people thrive in a changing environment and

can adapt to the change. After all, while my dad isn't parenting me in the same way as he was when I was a little girl, he's still an invaluable sounding board. Once I had had my moment of realization, my mentor explained that Sophie had joined when the business was a helpless baby, which she had helped to grow and thrive. She'd had all the cuddles and the kisses, and loved every moment of it. The needs of the business had been specific to her skill set and enthusiasms. But now the business was a surly teenager and Sophie was finding it difficult to cope. She wanted to go back to bringing up that cute toddler, but of course the business could no more turn back time than a teenager can.

We couldn't stop the business from growing, but nor could we stop Sophie from wanting to work somewhere better suited to her, either. It wasn't about what we did, or who we were, it was about the stage that the business was at. Some people just love those early days – the mucking in, sharing rooms and sleeping on sofas at consumer shows, no one with a proper job description yet, everything to play for. At the other end of the scale, there are some people who wince at the potential for chaos and lack of infrastructure in those toddler days!

We had tried to keep Sophie on by flexing the business around her, but ultimately it wasn't going to work. We would all have been doing the equivalent of trying to deny a teenager their first steps at independence – keeping them in romper suits and playing with teddy bears!

We had to accept the change, and it was such a relief when we realized that this was behind the issues Sophie was having. We could now see that she was the equivalent of a brilliant primary-school teacher, with the sort of patience and attention to detail needed to teach a five-year-old those first steps to reading, but she was now effectively in a bustling secondary school where moody teens were asking difficult questions and answering back.

No one would expect a devoted primary-school teacher to stay in that secondary-school environment – it's not what they'd signed up for – and so we realized that it was the right time for Sophie to leave. Things weren't going to 'go back to how they were'. We all have days when we wish we could have that cuddly baby back in our arms, but it's not going to happen no matter how much you will it. I'm so glad that we tried, though, as Sophie could leave on good terms, with us all knowing that we'd done our best; we'd simply hit a situation we couldn't change.

As a business begins to mature, it often needs new or different people to manage it. Leadership styles might change, branding might have a tune-up, and staff may come and go. But you can't change the way a growing – and thriving – business is run in order to mould it around someone who wants to be in a different type of company altogether. We've kept to the same values, but we've changed a lot. Sophie, who wanted a different set-up, found a smaller company before long and felt comfortable again. And, with no hard feelings, we continued to change and develop.

The Takeaway

Some businesses grow and change faster than the people within them. Be prepared to let people move on if they can't handle the change – after all, as with teachers, the same job in a different environment is sometimes a change too far! Keep these points in mind:

- Businesses might grow up, but some staff won't (or can't) grow with the business.
- Don't change the business to suit just one person.

The Task

As you read this, you may still be in the 'new baby' stage with your business and at this point it's very difficult to imagine how the next stages will look and how they might impact you and your team. So for some of you this is a task that will have to wait until your business begins to grow.

Communication is key to preparing for and managing change, so as your staff numbers swell make time to check in with your original staff, the stalwarts, the ones who have been with you from the earliest days, and give them the opportunity to express how they feel about how the business is changing and how that affects them and their original role.

It's important to give people the opportunity to talk about how things used to be and how they are now, without them worrying about being judged by others or having their comments taken as criticisms. This will build a stronger team going forward, even if some of your 'original' group make the decision to move on to pastures new.

> **Sara says:**
>
> **You don't need a crystal ball to know that in life and in business the one thing that's guaranteed is change.**

Lesson 40
Everest

**If you want to climb Everest,
get the best guides.**

THE STORY

I create products that sell through demonstration: I *show* the customer how my product can help solve a problem they often didn't realize they had. I know I'm the best in the world at selling craft products on television – I call it 'selling the sizzle, not the sausage'. But I'm not naive enough to think that I'm also the best at everything else.

A few years ago we decided we needed to increase our 'on-shelf' sales. These sales come from products stocked in stores, in a tub or a box on the shelf, next to a lot of other similar products. In contrast to TV and demo-driven sales, on-shelf sales happen when the customer simply comes across the product, static, without any engagement from me or Crafter's Companion. With these sales we just have to hope that our products are the ones to catch the customer's eye; there is far less we can do when we aren't there ourselves to persuade them to buy.

Despite stocking on-shelf ranges for years, we had never really done very well with them, and I was struggling to work out why. I'm always looking for opportunities to bring my products to life, so I was determined to broaden our customer base and get things shifting in this area.

I talked to some of our existing customers and realized that the stuff they bought off the shelf was marketed in a completely different way to the stock they ordered from us after seeing a demonstration. This was a light-bulb moment: I needed to rethink the retailing strategy. But at this point it really did feel like being in the foothills of Everest – the task seemed that huge, and I didn't know where to start. I could have immediately thrown myself into trying to learn this completely different way of marketing – but just as I knew I *could* climb a mountain if I really, truly set my mind to it, I also knew I wouldn't even consider it without the very best guide out there. So instead of trying to climb this marketing mountain alone, I hired the best in the business: a select group of people who were already doing exactly what I wanted to do, only for other companies.

Before long, we had developed a new product range, with new naming, new packaging and a new price point. It was a completely separate product portfolio from the one we sold via TV, and one I could never have put together without my trusty guides.

Sales took off and it taught me a very important lesson: if you want to do something new, look at what works already and find out who's doing it. We now employ two completely separate teams working two very different business models – the 'on-shelf' team and the 'demonstrations' one – and the results speak for themselves.

There's one important caveat here. You'll remember we've already talked about hiring staff who have the right attitude or personality for your organization, and that still stands. No excuses for round pegs in square holes, please! Let's put it this way: yes, you want the best guide to get you up Everest, but you still have to pick someone that you could handle being halfway up a mountain with when you're starving hungry, missing your family and wondering if you'll ever make it. Expertise alone will only get you so far.

The Takeaway

If you have a mountain to climb, get yourself some guides. You'll reach your destination quicker and won't get lost along the route. Also remember to:

- find out what other people are doing 'right', especially among your competitors
- consider hiring experts as they can be more effective and cheaper than trying to learn from scratch
- build a network of experts so you can access the knowledge you need quickly

The Task

This week's task is about being ready when opportunities (and challenges) come knocking! I want you to think about the areas of expertise that you and your company may need to access, then go about creating your 'little black book' of contacts that you can call upon when needed. This isn't a task that you can sit down and complete in an hour or two, it's going to be an ongoing process that you add to and refine over time. But the rewards will be significant – being able to draw on a team just when you need it will make you more responsive than your competitors and more able to adapt to change. Whether it's a good builder, a great marketing agency or a fab catering company, knowing you can get them involved in a project will give you the confidence to go out and seize those opportunities.

"

Sara says:

There aren't many occasions in business when you are a true pioneer – there are other people who have climbed Everest – so don't be blind to the opportunity to fast-track your learning by following in the footsteps of what already works.

"

Lesson 41
Make Time for Reflection

Never underestimate the importance of hindsight when moving forwards.

THE STORY

We've talked about the importance of rest and reflection in an earlier lesson and I'm going to stress it again – but this time I want you to be thinking about taking accountability for your growth. This lesson is a pause for you to go back and reflect on any of the lessons we've discussed so far that you might have rushed through.

Believe me, I know how it gets. All it takes is a sick child, parent or employee and the week can unravel pretty sharpish. The best-laid plans can turn to dust when confronted with a car that needs taking to the garage or a client issue that needs immediate prioritizing. So, of course I understand that by this stage in the book you may have had a week (or even two) when you just skim-read the lesson. Perhaps at 9 p.m. on a Sunday. Just so that you could tell yourself that you'd 'done' it. Or perhaps the lesson was addressing something that deep down you knew you should be taking seriously in your life and business but that felt a little uncomfortable at the time. Too confronting. Or just too much like hard work on top of everything else.

Well, I'm sorry – and pleased! – to say that this is the week you go back to that lesson. Read it again with fresh eyes and a couple of months of other learning behind you. Does it seem easier now? Have you had a perspective shift because of other changes you've made since? Or does it feel just as challenging but at least this time you've had a bit more sleep? I hope so.

Because by this point you've not only used your time and money to go out of your way and buy this book, but also – if you're taking it week-by-week – you've stuck with it for nine months. You have been investing in yourself all this time, as you deserve to. However, if you just picked it up on a whim and are trying to rush through it, catching up when you can, then you'll find that you very quickly start to forget what you've already learned – especially if you're not building in enough time to complete the tasks and put the things you've learned along the way into practice.

So, this week: stop. And reflect. And, if necessary, catch up. This is me telling you that you have to make yourself accountable for what you are trying to accomplish here.

Try telling someone close to you that this is a catch-up week rather than a 'week off', and ask them to check in with you. Or leave yourself a note in your diary so that you have to check in with yourself and how you've done by the end of the week. Either way, make sure that you make yourself accountable, otherwise your head will always only be half remembering what you should have learned – and the self-recrimination simply isn't worth it.

The Takeaway

Reflection is a rarely taught but powerful skill. Build time into your day to reflect, and make yourself accountable for your growth. Understand that reflection has the same importance as any other form of self-development. To get the most from the process:

- Reflect consciously and regularly.
- Be aware that reflection can be revealing and even uncomfortable – be open-minded and don't be defensive.

Sara Davies

The Task

One of the best ways to make a lesson really sink in is to write down what you took away from it and how it can help your business.

This week I want you to look back through the preceding lessons within this book. You can re-read all the lessons or just a selection of them, but I'd suggest that you aim for a minimum of seven. As you read, I want you to make notes on the pages, highlighting the key messages and takeaways that you feel have particular resonance. This process will help you reflect on the tasks you have completed and focus your mind on what you have learned from each of them.

66

Sara says:

I often scribble all over the books I'm reading – and I fold the pages over, too! This is a really good way to spotlight the key points and remind myself of the stuff that has really made an impact; it's a great way to self-mentor.

99

Lesson 42
The Unspoken Negative

**Everyone has a quibble – you just
have to be the first to spot it.**

THE STORY

During my training for shopping TV, I learned the concept of the 'unspoken negative'. Now I use it all the time to great effect, in business and beyond. In short, the technique involves working out what the person you're selling to might see as the negative in your pitch – a quibble, if you like – and then dealing with that negative during the pitch itself. Let me explain.

In almost every interaction that involves a sale, whether it's selling a product, an idea or a way of doing things, there will be a quibble. It's that little moment most of us have, just before we say yes to something, when we run a few checks internally to make sure that we really do want to commit.

So my tactic is to make sure I've dealt with any of these internal checks, or quibbles, before my customer has had the chance to confront me with it themselves. But I need to be careful: in an effort to overcome a potential quibble, I don't want to draw attention to anything negative that the customer might not have thought of in the first place! If I'm talking to a retailer who is thinking of stocking my pens, I will of course want to big up all the features and benefits of the range – and hopefully this will draw extra attention to the packaging, design and marketing material, too. What I also need to do in this interaction is to figure out what the buyer's unspoken negative is, and to deal with it *before* they get a chance to raise it.

For example, perhaps I've done my research and I know that my pens are 25 per cent more expensive than the others stocked by this retailer. Therefore during my pitch I will slip in a line explaining that yes, I appreciate there is a price difference, but that's because the pens are made with only the finest brush nibs, sourced from Japan, which is known for making the best nibs in the world – but they're pricey. Most people just go to a pen factory wherever and ask for nibs, but we go a little further than that. This means that the quality is unparalleled, and as a result customers who use them have a better experience and consistently return to repurchase.

All of a sudden, whoever I am pitching to is no longer dwelling on the quibble they might have had but is instead focusing on the knowledge that this is a product that will create repeat customers for them. And how is that not a win?

Obviously this is a great strategy in a straight sales pitch, but I also use it a lot in my role as a business leader. Really, it's once again a matter of staying connected to your empathy for other people's concerns, whether they are buyers, investors or employees. For example, if I'm holding a town hall and speaking to all the staff internally about a big change or forthcoming new range, I'll make sure that I've set aside some time to reflect on what might cause anxiety about the news. I'll want them to know when I introduce it that I have considered what the change might mean for them, that I have put things in place to make sure they're not negatively impacted – that I *care*.

The Takeaway

Every customer will have an unspoken negative that could stop them from buying from you or using your services. If you can work out what that unspoken negative is, and deal with it before they even mention it, then you make it much easier for them to say 'yes'. Here's a quibble checklist:

- Everyone has potential quibbles.
- Work out what unspoken negatives a customer might have.
- Develop strategies to overcome the quibbles.

The Task

This week's task is to help you overcome any potential unspoken negatives. I want you to take a look at your main product pitch. Then imagine a specific buyer, customer or business partner, and write down below what their three key unspoken negatives might be:

1.

2.

3.

Now think about how you might address these potential unspoken negatives. What could you say to help overcome them? You could even record yourself pitching your product to the person you have in mind and play it back to see how well you handle the potential negatives. Or try it out on

family and friends. How would you rate yourself
out of ten? Repeat the process a couple more times,
each time looking to improve, until you feel
comfortable that you can address them with
confidence.

"

Sara says:

**If people do have quibbles, it's because they've
been thinking about what you are 'selling'
them – visualizing what it would be like if they
went ahead. So, to me, that quibble is actually a
sign of interest, rather than a negative.**

"

Lesson 43
The 55/38/7 Formula

Never forget the importance of body language.

THE STORY

I always believed that body language was important, but it was working on *Dragons' Den* that really made me see that it's crucial. You can get so much done before you even say a word! And it's not just me who thinks so. Albert Mehrabian, a professor of psychology, came up with the famous breakdown of the components of face-to-face conversation. A specialist in body language, he found that when we communicate, only 7 per cent of meaning comes through the words we say; 38 per cent is through the tone of our voice and a staggering 55 per cent is nonverbal. According to him (and now many more people), the vast majority of communication is nonverbal. This might feel hard to grasp but once you have got your head around it, it can actually make meetings, presentations and even public appearances feel easier, rather than more difficult.

When entrepreneurs come into the Den, the lift opens and we five Dragons are all sitting there, facing them, rather than looking at each other. From the minute that person sees us, they have our full attention and, crucially, we have theirs. We can't hide behind each other. We are on show, even when we're not speaking.

I am very conscious that I may not be the first to speak to the entrepreneur. They present their business first of all, and then one of the other Dragons might jump in and speak before me. But as far as I'm concerned, when that happens, absolutely none of that time is going to waste. In fact, I am making great use of it. For starters, I make sure that I don't have 'resting bitch face', and that I look engaged and empathetic no matter how badly their initial pitch might be going and no matter how cripplingly nervous they might be.

On top of this, I make sure that I almost over-exaggerate my body language. I force myself to face them, even if I'm feeling fidgety or uncomfortable. Heels or no heels, I make sure I don't shift about, remaining visibly engaged. I ferociously nod at points they make so that they know I am actively listening, and I'm overt in paying attention to certain points when I take notes. My communication is nonverbal at this point but it is definite, confident communication nonetheless.

Next I make sure that when I do open my mouth, irrespective of my words, I present myself with a soft, positive tone. Imagine how stressful it must be to be one of those entrepreneurs. You must hardly be able to take in what's being said to you, especially when all of us start chipping in, adding further facts and figures. What will shine through is the impression I give through how I hold myself and what my tone is. And I can get that in before any of the other Dragons gets a word in. So I do.

On my second-ever day in the Den, I remember, the first investment of the morning was two women who came in with a fantastic pitch. I was so into them from the get-go, and I was making sure that I came across as positive. Thank heavens, because that day all of us were going for it – every single Dragon was keen. But no one knew me! These were entrepreneurs who had never seen me on the show as none of my episodes had aired yet. I had no credibility in their eyes; I was just the random new woman.

But they chose me. Why? Well, my offer wasn't that different from any of the other Dragons', but they said in the antechamber later on that they just felt they hit it off with me. It was instinct as much as anything else. And what made them feel this? I'm pretty sure it was the hard work I had put in with my body language – I had already said a lot before I even started speaking.

The Takeaway

Your body is a powerful way of conveying your thoughts and feelings without saying a word. Just as you spent years developing speech, you should now commit to practising nonverbal communication. Use these key methods:

- Pay attention to other people's body language, and note what they're conveying.
- Learn to control and modify your own body language to convey the message that *you* want to present.

The Task

Being able to read and respond to body language is a great skill to develop. While some of you may not get face-to-face with customers and suppliers very often, I still think it's a skill you need if you want to succeed in business.

So this week, in your next meeting, I'd like you to focus on both your own body language and that of other people in the room. What is it telling you?

If you don't have any face-to-face meetings, then focus on body language in a social situation. It can be fascinating to watch the body language of a couple in a restaurant or bar; you might not be able to hear the conversation but you should be able to gather lots of information about their relationship from their body language alone.

To enhance your ability to interpret body language, I'd also strongly recommend that you read up on the subject. There are lots of great books on this – a quick google will reveal some options, but you might take a look at *The Definitive Book of Body Language* by Allan and Barbara Pease, *What Every Body Is Saying* by Joe Navarro and Marvin Karlins, or Albert Mehrabian's *Nonverbal Communication*.

> ❝
>
> *Sara says:*
>
> **Wherever possible, I like to communicate face-to-face as it gives me the opportunity to present my messages more vividly. So, it's 'camera on' for all my online meetings and I make an effort to look into the lens of the monitor, rather than looking at the faces on the screen. This makes the viewers feel that I'm making eye-contact and has a bigger impact.**
>
> ❞

Lesson 44
Anyone for Tea?

When a cuppa is about more than a cuppa.

THE STORY

A few years ago I hired a real hotshot at Crafter's Companion. He was absolutely fantastic at what he did; we'd had to go all out to persuade him to come and work for us, and we gave him a great salary because he produced great results. In fact, he was the first person we had on the staff who was earning more than me!

But – and you knew there would be a 'but', didn't you? – after a few months I began to pick up on an increasing edginess between him and some of the other staff, particularly those junior to him. I just couldn't work out what the root of the problem was, though – he was genuinely a nice guy, to everyone, and he was great at his job. He wasn't a 'square peg in a round hole'. I kept an eye on the situation for a bit, and before long I noticed that unlike everyone else in the office, he never did a tea round.

So what?, you might think. But the tea round is a big tradition in our office. *Everyone* makes tea from time to time – *for everyone*. To this day, Simon and I will still pop the kettle on and make a brew now and then. And it's not just about the tea. Of course, we all love a cuppa, but it's more than that. It's about showing that we still see ourselves as a team, that we still care about each other, that we're prepared to go out of our way occasionally to do something beyond what needs to get done that day.

There was only one thing for it. I called him in to have a word. I asked him straight out if there was a reason why he never offered to make the tea, and explained that I was concerned that it was starting to wind some people up. To my surprise, he explained immediately: it wasn't that he didn't want to or he couldn't be bothered, but that he was painfully aware that he had come in and commanded a large salary. So much so that he didn't want senior management to see him being paid a lot of money per hour to be standing by the kettle or checking on how many sugars people took. In his mind, he was there to do a certain job, and he would have been mortified if it had looked as if he wasn't doing it.

He had a great point. He was expensive, and he would have been more productive away from the kettle. But there was a consequence more serious than a financial one to him not making tea: his team had started to see him as arrogant, as someone who thought he was above small acts of kindness for others. And now he was losing respect.

His actions said, 'I'm too important, so I'm above making tea', whether that was what he'd intended by them or not. To me, they also implied that he hadn't clocked the senior management also pulling their weight at the tea station. Us getting stuck in was a way of indicating that he should, too, but he'd failed to observe that. And for a company like ours, it wouldn't do. So I told him he needed to start making the occasional tea round. He did, and it was horrible tea, but it improved relations no end.

What I took from the experience was that we should have made our values as a company clearer to him. None of us had considered that he may have come from a highly corporate role where dallying around in the kitchen could have seen him lose a huge amount of sway internally. What he'd needed to do was look around him and read the room. Wherever you're working, you do need to modify your habits a little. You need to understand the values of your place of business and run your day according to those values.

Yes, they were expensive cups of tea when he made

them. But yes, they were worth it to see the team come together and the company now happy and productive.

The Takeaway

Never assume that everyone understands your company culture; you have to continually walk the talk and be clear about what makes your company different. It's too easy to lose sight of how important the small stuff is, so keep on top of it. See the following as mantras for this:

- What you do is as important as what you say.
- Lead by example.

The Task

This week's task is to think about your company culture. Ask yourself the questions: 'Does my company/business have a recognizable culture?'; 'Is it an unsaid thing or is it written down in the shape of a company-values statement?' Even if you're only a two-person team, ask yourself: 'Are we both on the same page when it comes to how we want to operate?'

If your culture isn't clear then take the time to formalize and communicate it, and check in regularly to make sure it's still relevant and understood by everyone.

> *Sara says:*
>
> When it comes to instilling a culture in a company, regardless of its size, communication and consistency are absolutely key.

Lesson 45
Chameleons

Chameleons change colour . . . but they never stop being chameleons.

THE STORY

There is nothing more disheartening than realizing, in the middle of a pitch, that someone isn't paying attention to what you're saying. As you know, I spend my life reading body language and I can spot that lack of attention pretty quickly these days, which means I'm just as quick to intervene – and my methods aren't what you might expect.

From my earliest experiences demonstrating products at local craft shows, to key business presentations and even *Dragons' Den*, I've always kept an eye on what people are expressing through their body language – often, it can be a more honest expression of how they feel than the words they choose to use! As a salesperson, reading the room through body language is an essential skill; you need to be able to respond to the mood – and fast, as your sales depend on it!

In the past, if the audience appeared to be drifting off I might have tried to break people out of their 'trance' by saying more dramatic things, or making more of my own body language – trying to take up more of the room, if you will. But I've learned from my TV training that this isn't necessarily the key to recapturing attention.

What you need is not to do more of something or to change your character completely – after all, there's nothing worse than looking or feeling as if you're trying too hard; most audiences will sniff out inauthenticity – or worse still, desperation – faster than anything else. Instead, the trick is to add some light and shade. When I'm presenting on shopping TV, I imagine I'm on the TV in the corner of someone's living room while they're doing some vacuuming or crochet, or whatever. They only have one eye on the screen while I'm chatting away. Instead of getting louder, or faster, incrementally raising the pressure, it works better to simply pause, or to go very quiet; a break in the expected.

Sara Davies

Immediately, it's human instinct to look up. *Is something wrong? Where has the noise gone?* Your viewer will snap to attention.

Then – *BAM!* – it's time to make your most important point, just as you have their full focus.

I'm not talking about bringing anything inauthentic to your pitch. This technique is about changing the presentation, not changing who you are. After all, a chameleon is still a chameleon even when they're adapting to their surroundings. You're being true to yourself but you're being smart for your audience. And they might not even notice how much more they're noticing.

The Takeaway

Don't blame your audience if they're drifting off; instead, take responsibility for keeping them engaged. It's fine to change your presentation style to win the audience. Keep these points in mind:

- Be flexible in how you connect with your audience.
- Stick to your vision but don't become a slave to your planned delivery – you can still be true to yourself and your message.
- If what you are doing isn't working, change it.

The Task

This week's task is to have a laugh. Seriously, take some time to laugh out loud. Why? Because some of the best presenters are comedians. Even though they will have a carefully crafted routine worked out before they set foot on-stage, the very best ones will be able to change and adapt their routine in response to the audience. They call it ad libbing, and my goodness they can be brilliant at it. So you have my full permission to settle down and search out your favourite stand-up routines on YouTube – all I ask you to do in between the laughs is take the time to appreciate the chameleon-like abilities of the performer!

"

Sara says:

When you watch a great comedian (my choice would be Peter Kay), look and listen for the pauses – the moments they glance back at the audience, waiting for the room to be ready, then deliver the punchline. Comic timing is as much about the pause as the punchline – and in business, too, timing can be everything.

"

Lesson 46

Turn Your Customers into Your Marketeers

Connecting with your customers on a personal level can create good vibes – and so much more.

THE STORY

Whatever your business, it's important to talk to your customers – to find out what drives them, what makes them feel valued, what they're saying to each other. I've enjoyed doing this at craft fairs all of my life, and I'm also partial to popping into our retail stores – seeing who's in there and having a bit of a chat with them. As I've already mentioned in Lesson 35, 'Keeping Your Tank Topped Up', these interactions keep your tank topped up and can keep you fizzing with energy, reminding you why you got into your chosen industry. And the good news is that on top of that, it just makes cracking business sense!

As my career and the company have developed, so has social media. These days we have a huge social media community and I take a lot of time to be active in our groups, seeing what people have been making and giving compliments when things catch my eye.

There is nothing that makes me smile as much as seeing a new crafter posting their first item with a nervous explanation that it's for a new grandchild's christening or it's a birthday card for a friend they haven't seen for a while, only for the comments to start flowing beneath the image – a stream of congratulations and warm wishes.

Thousands more customers see those comments in turn, and they then spread the positivity even further with their own responses, all while giving further crafters the confidence to post their own creations. Obviously this all has a huge feel-good factor to it, but it also turns our own customers into an essential part of our marketing team. People who develop a passion for crafting and who are able to express their love for their friends and family via their creations are the very best ambassadors we could ever have – and they absolutely love talking about what they've made and how they've done it.

So, never think about connecting with other people this way as merely 'feeding back' or 'connecting with the client base' but as a genuine human interaction. People care about how they express themselves, and in our case we're giving them the very best tools to do that. But for any business, making these sincere connections can lead to so much more, because if you can create that feel-good factor in customers – with either products or the way that you interact with them – then they will tell other people. People want to talk about their positive experiences, and if they share with their networks, then their networks become yours. When treated with respect and empathy, customers can become your marketing department's greatest asset.

The Takeaway

Actively seek out your customers, engage in their conversations and listen to what they say. They will refocus, energize and inspire you, and they can help to spread that positivity wider. To make the most of this valuable input:

- Make it easy to talk to and listen to your customers.

- Create communities and groups where customers can become advocates for your company.

The Task

This week I want you to think about how you can leverage social media to engage with your customers.

Do some basic market research:

- Ask customers which social media platform they most commonly use.
- Ask whether they use it to search for products or people, or do they just browse for leisure?

These are important questions as there's no point investing huge amounts of time and money on an Instagram account if your customers are mainly Facebook users!

If you have staff, then talk to them about their ideas – you may have some social-media-savvy experts right under your nose. Your IT guy might love producing DIY content for YouTube or your junior accountant might be a TikTok sensation. Also look at other businesses in your field: see what they are doing and who's doing it well.

Then you have what you need to develop a social media strategy that is both manageable and measurable. Consider the frequency of your posts and remember that social media is a very visual tool, so focus on images and video content where possible, keeping the word count to a minimum.

"

Sara says:

There are lots of ways in which you can use social media, but you need to be careful that it doesn't just hoover up your time and money for very little return, so keep an eye on what benefits it's delivering.

"

Lesson 47
Stepping Away

Absence makes the business beat stronger.

THE STORY

I always knew that taking time out from the business to have children would change things. I just couldn't be completely sure what might change, or how. Would the business collapse without me? Would I lose my touch? Would I develop new skills I'd never even known I had?

As it happened, it wasn't just me who changed immeasurably, it was also my team.

In those early newborn days, I was so worried about letting down the business by not being there enough. What if something went wrong? I knew that there were plans and structures in place – and I knew Simon was there, too, even if he was a little bleary-eyed from the night-feed disturbances!

I managed to get ahold of my anxieties, though, and took a decent chunk of time off for each baby, just about holding myself back from constantly phoning in to check up on things. Then, when I did return, I understood that not only had there been no need to worry, but that the team had actually grown stronger in my absence.

One thing in particular had changed: people had grown used to making decisions by themselves. When I left for maternity leave, there had still been a culture in the company of people waiting for my final say before making any decisions. Whether I was out for the day or away on holiday, things got put to one side, waiting for me to give the go-ahead.

You know what it's like: if you take a week off, it can feel as if you're coming back to a full week's work in your inbox when you've barely switched on your computer. People tend not to account for the fact that you're not there; they know you'll be back soon or that you might even be checking in. They know there's a limit to what can mount up in your absence, it's only a week or so after all. So they 'keep you in the loop', the list of tasks steadily building while you're on the beach.

It's similar to parenting itself. You don't expect your baby to suddenly get up and walk one day; you have to let them topple over a few times. And when they're older, if you bring your kids home from school and follow them into the house picking up their shoes, coats, bags behind them, you'll end up with a family who doesn't pick up after themselves. But if you remind your kids that those pegs in the hallway have a function, as they throw their coats on the floor (which they will always try and get away with every now and again!), you will end up with a family who do their fair share in the home. I'm not expecting miracles; no one gives a six-year-old a kitchen knife and asks them to start preparing dinner! It's about offering considered doses of independence and responsibility in order to help them develop even more of it.

Being away from the office for longer stretches of time – for example, during maternity leave or on a sabbatical – is the ultimate example of this. It doesn't allow for that 'Oh, they'll be back after the weekend' mentality. It is too long for issues to be left, undecided and uncompleted, but it is long enough for people to develop a new skill: making decisions for themselves.

I get it. Nobody wants to be the one who has reorganized things while the boss went on a mini-break, only to be told on the boss's return that it was totally inappropriate for them to have done so. But being absent for a longer time allows for something different, something even more productive. When your absence creates a space, others can grow into that space, thinking for themselves without expecting you to be back in the driving seat soon. Perhaps it's the renewed sense of independence, or perhaps it's as simple as the fact that they know it's *they* who will be dealing with the consequences of their decisions, not you. But one thing is for sure, absence really is an opportunity for people to grow.

The Takeaway

A business can grow only to a limited size if it is entirely dependent on one person being constantly at the centre of it, making every call, every day. With me stepping away long enough for the team to learn to make their own decisions, not only did the business continue to grow but the team's collective heart was able to beat all the stronger. Two top tips on this:

- Don't stifle growth by micromanaging everything.
- Give people the space to think and act for themselves.

The Task

This week I want you to write down five items that are on your 'To do' list – they can be work or personal tasks, but they need to be ones that could possibly be delegated. So, if you're a 'one-man band' in business with no one to delegate to, you'll be better off focusing on non-work-related jobs!

1.

2.

3.

4.

5.

Once you have your list, think about who could help you complete them – whose skills might be well-suited and how you might ask them. They don't have to be big tasks – it could be as simple as picking the kids up from school, putting on a wash or getting a meal ready. This isn't about dumping a task on someone who really doesn't want to do it, it's about understanding what you can let other people help out with and about asking for their help. Some people go through life unable to delegate the simplest of tasks and often end up spreading themselves too thinly and being quite stressed! Delegation should become a healthy habit, not a rare occurrence, so make sure you consciously practise doing it.

> **Sara says:**
>
> We all want to feel needed, which is why many of us find delegation difficult, so be conscious of your own ego and focus on what will work best for the business by taking the emotion out of delegation.

Lesson 48
Developing the Next Generation

Make Ashleigh a leader, so Ashleigh can create more Ashleighs.

THE STORY

It's easy to slip into a mindset that focuses only on sales and margins as the keys to growing your company, but one of the most effective ways to build your business is to develop your staff – *and retain them*. It's called succession planning, which sounds very grand but is actually quite simple – even if it can be surprisingly challenging to persuade your staff that this is the case.

In short, succession planning is all about preparing people to move up in the company by getting them to develop and mentor their replacement. How might that be a bad thing? Well, it sounds simple enough but in practice it can involve some delicate interpersonal negotiating because what you're actually asking staff members to do is to train up staff below them, ready to move up into their role.

When you put it like that, of course it becomes clear why people don't always respond well! They're already doing that role, so why would they want to be creating a replacement person to do their job? That's the way people often see it, and it can make them feel insecure, paranoid and worried about the implications for their own future.

So, you need to explain the plan clearly from the outset. Take, for example, one of my employees, Ashleigh. She came to me when she was in her mid-twenties and started out at Crafter's Companion as a marketing and PR executive. It was obvious that she was very talented and someone I wanted to keep in the company. If you find someone brilliant, of course you don't want to lose them. And what I have learned is that the key to keeping these people is not just to clear space for them to move up into, but to help them train up people below them precisely so that they have the freedom to make that move upwards. The reality is, you're going to move up faster if you can also backfill your own role.

I could have just forged a path for Ashleigh myself to

allow her to move upwards in the business, something she probably would have done anyway. But then, five years later, I would only have had one Ashleigh. By persuading her that she needed to teach the more junior staff the skills they would need to eventually move up themselves, I have now effectively got several Ashleighs in the company. All are on different levels, and all have been persuaded to keep training up those below them.

Most people are resistant to this idea at first – especially if they've had negative experiences in the past. It's not an unreasonable response to feel defensive, to assume that they're going to do themselves out of a job, and this is why I've invested so much in building trust with my staff. Words are hollow: there's no point in telling people you've got a great plan if they believe there's a chance they really might end up out of a job in a couple of months' time, so you can't just tell people that you don't want to lose them or that it isn't a threat to invest in the staff below. You have to demonstrate to them how it has worked in the past, to point out to them what you have done with others and how those people are now flying.

Simply telling them that you're preparing their course upwards in the company is not enough. You have to show them that it's possible – that you're making sure that there are opportunities for them to move up so, of course, they'll be expected to do the same for the more junior staff. It's about development, not disposability. Asking your staff to engage in succession planning is a compliment – it means that you never want to lose them, not that you're planning to!

The Takeaway

Developing talent from within can be very cost-effective and it creates loyalty and opportunity for existing staff. Create a succession plan for staff so that they can embrace the opportunity this brings. In particular:

- Reassure staff of their value; explain that you want to retain them.
- Show how you're developing their replacement so they will be free to move up.

The Task

Your task is to develop a buddy system. Buddy systems are where two employees are put together so they can learn from each other. They work particularly well when you buddy-up an experienced member of staff with someone new to a role and are a great way of transferring skills so that you can all grow together. Buddy systems also build new relationships and give a clear point of contact for new starters when they need help or advice. Exposure to the more experienced 'buddy', and seeing them perform in a role that the less experienced 'buddy' may aspire to, also helps new employees to think about their career growth.

If you already have some staff, then the buddy system is also a brilliant method of succession planning, getting more experienced employees to help develop the person that can fill their boots when it's time for them to move onwards and upwards in the company.

If you don't have staff then you can apply the same principles of the buddy system to suppliers and customers, helping them to grow and develop, and making those relationships more valuable as those contacts become more senior and influential within their own companies.

"

Sara says:

You never know where a client might end up. The person you met as an office junior can become a senior buyer or the managing director. Investing in those relationships and helping them to develop can pay huge dividends.

"

Lesson 49
When Good People Want to Leave

If you love them, let them go.

THE STORY

I can convince anyone of anything. Simon rolls his eyes when I say this, but I'm sure of it. It might sound like a fantastic gift, but let me tell you: the hardest part of all is realizing when the best thing to do is *not* to convince people of something. That's the real knack.

For example, from time to time one of my team will come to me saying, 'Sara, Denise in Sales has said they're leaving. They've been offered a job elsewhere. Please have a word with them, as we really need to keep them.' Under normal circumstances, I know exactly how this will pan out. I'll talk things through with them, I'll work out what package is needed to convince them to stay, and then they'll stay. But sometimes that's not the best thing to do.

A while back, we had a fantastic young woman in our marketing team. She was a real asset to the business, as well as being a lovely person with great values. I thought we were a wonderful fit, until she came to me and explained that she had been offered the chance to become a wedding planner. It was a real surprise that she was looking to leave as I had thought things were going brilliantly, but I remembered that right back when she joined the company she had mentioned her long-term dream of one day becoming a wedding planner. At the time she said it, she didn't seem to think it was even a possibility, but now it was – a solid job offer.

I knew I could try to convince her to stay – and I very much wanted her to stay. But I also knew it would have been wrong, not just for me and for her, but for the wider company. Because there would always have been a 'What if?' for her. Even if she'd stayed and continued to do a cracking job, there would always have been that question mark at the back of her mind. What else could she have been? Resentment could have trickled in, and that can be contagious. No one should feel that I have been the one to benefit from their career choices rather than them. No one should ever be thinking, *I wonder what would have happened . . . if not for Sara Davies.* I know I would still be thinking the same about any boss who had stood in my path to my own dream career.

This young woman could never have become a wedding planner in my company; the lines of progression simply weren't there for her. So I congratulated her and explained that of course she should follow her dream. I also told her that she would be sorely missed and that while I couldn't keep her job open for her, that I would always welcome her back if things didn't work out.

I knew that it was the right thing to do. I only want people to stay if it's the right thing for them as well as for us – it should never be just about buying people up. After all, there's no point in having a company filled with staff who have the very best qualifications and skills but who are all dreaming of being elsewhere. Like it or not, it'll catch up with you in the long term.

The Takeaway

It's important to do the right thing for the individuals who work for you, even if in the short term it can cause disruption to you or the company. Keeping people who are ready to leave never works out; let them go, wish them well and you never know, one day you may find yourself working together again. For things to go smoothly:

- Put yourself in the leaver's shoes – understand their reasons.
- Base your actions on how you would like to be treated.

The Task

This week's task is a combination of self-reflection and planning for the future.

I want you to think about how you might handle a resignation. In virtually every business people will come and go, and it's important to let them leave without resentment on either side, which is where an 'exit poll' can be really useful.

An 'exit interview' is not about trying to trick them into staying – far from it. It's about respecting an individual's reasons for leaving and, as a company, gathering potential lessons. Take the time to talk to employees when they leave, in a non-confrontational way, asking for their feedback about what they found challenging while working for your company and what they would change. This information can be invaluable!

At the end of the 'exit interview' make sure you thank your employee for what they have done so they'll give your business a positive review – you never know where they'll end up!

> 66
>
> *Sara says:*
>
> **Resignations can feel a bit like a divorce, but you need to understand that they're rarely personal – it's just a natural consequence of building a business.**
>
> 99

Lesson 50
Don't Treat Your Staff Like Family Members

Family is family, and work is work.

THE STORY

I've often heard the phrase 'Oh, we're like one big family here' thrown around in business environments and I must admit it makes me a little uneasy. I grew up as part of a family business, and I now work alongside my husband, so I am sure I've got the qualifications to speak on this one. And it's a real bugbear of mine, because I think too many bosses actually use the idea of 'being like a family' as a short cut to treating staff badly.

Your family are your family, either through birth, marriage or choice. You can't pay them to spend time

277

with you. Being a sibling, cousin or auntie isn't a profession, so if you remove necessity from the equation and you haven't built strong bonds, they simply won't turn up if they don't want to! But whether you all get along or not, family is who they are, and even if you live far apart, they'll probably keep cropping up a few times a year regardless.

But staff are *contracted* to turn up and get the job done. They're there because I pay them to be there. Yes, I want them to do their best and to love their time at work. I'd like everyone who works for me to feel that they're not just *doing* a great job but that they *have* a great job. They shouldn't feel like a reluctant or unwelcome guest – far from it. But it's important to remember the relationship is a transactional one.

It's equally important to remember that some family members will never want to feel like an employee; they're family, and to feel like any other employee wouldn't sit comfortably with them.

The nature of most companies is that when they were small start-ups, a significant number of those helping out will have been family – and they will have played a part in getting the company off the ground *because* they were family. In my case, it was my dad giving me advice and endless lifts, my sister blow-drying the sawdust off the early Envelopers and packing them up for us, and even my mam chipping in with whatever was needed. They wanted me to succeed, so they were doing what they could. But they were definitely acting as family, not employees, who wouldn't and shouldn't just put up with anything I throw at them – even if my mam and dad did.

As soon as your company starts to grow, if you're still relying on family and favours from staff, resentments can start to appear. If money is flowing in and family don't feel fairly remunerated – especially if the whole enterprise would never have got going without them in the first place – problems can really mount up. Similarly, if you hire staff but still expect of them the same wild, unpaid hours and unpredictable workflow that your family may have tolerated in those exciting early days, they will also start to feel resentful – with good reason!

It's a question of setting and maintaining sensible boundaries. I'm not saying that you should never work with family. The hypocrisy if I did! And nor am I saying that you shouldn't create a company that is family-friendly, or even one that has the sense of warmth and camaraderie that most people associate with family. But you should never start to refer to your business as a family. All it will lead to in the long run is an erosion of the boundaries between two totally separate relationships.

The way to make your family feel valued if they're

helping you out as a favour is with your time, your love and your thanks. Then, if they end up working with you in the longer term, a fair salary needs to be added into the equation. And the way to make your employees feel valued is with a decent salary and decent working conditions. If they end up becoming friends for life, or even family, then lavish your time and love on them outside of working hours.

The Takeaway

Know the difference between family and employees. Don't take advantage of either relationship and reward each of them accordingly. Bear in mind that:

- some family members will never want to be treated as employees
- some employees will feel uncomfortable in a company that behaves like a family

The Task

This week's task is a combination of self-reflection and action. There are some elements of the task that are aimed at those with family involved in the business and others that are aimed at those who don't have family involved in the business.

Start by asking yourself the following questions:

- Have you ever had, or do you currently have, family or friends involved in your business?
- Was or is the relationship with them different from the one you would expect with an employee?

It's good to establish how any family or friends working for you feel about the business and their role in it, so ask them the following and listen carefully to their responses:

1. Do they see themselves as part of the business, or are they 'helping out', perhaps taking the view that their involvement is less formal than that of a regular employee?
2. Where do they see themselves in the business as it develops?
3. Are they ambitious for the company or are they cautious about where they would fit in if it became a larger organization?

This is not about making big decisions about the future, it's about understanding their view of where they sit in the bigger picture and checking your thinking is aligned. It's important to understand, and potentially manage, their expectations and aspirations when factoring them into any future plans.

If your business doesn't involve any family members or friends, there's still a lot to be gained by actively discussing with employees – especially those in the most senior roles – where they feel they sit in the future development of the business. Ask them questions 2 and 3 from the above list. Bear in mind that there are no right or wrong answers, and it's important to recognize that their responses are about their career path and aren't personal about you or your business. Remember, knowledge is key to effective and harmonious staff management.

> ❝
>
> *Sara says:*
>
> **It's important to define boundaries and work within them. Don't assume that everyone has the same view about their role as you do.**
>
> ❞

Lesson 51
Good Business Shape

How keeping in shape helps keep the business in good shape.

THE STORY

We all know that the list of reasons to keep yourself fit and healthy are as long as my arm – we're well aware of the mental health benefits, we're well warned about the risks of not doing any exercise and we all know how much better we feel when we put the effort in. But sometimes that doesn't help to motivate us and just adds to the pressure to work out, on top of pressures elsewhere. But in my case, what I hadn't realized was how good keeping fit would be for the business itself. Not until lockdown, that is.

Sara Davies

Everyone has their 'thing' when it comes to fitness, whether it's weights or swimming or Pilates. My preference is running – by a mile! I started about five or six years ago and it was only really because my doctor told me that I needed to do it for my own fitness and weight loss. I didn't expect much; it was just something that had to be done.

To my surprise it ended up getting me through one of my toughest challenges – and I'm not talking about running a marathon, but about lockdown. Of course, I love getting that blast of fresh air and feeling fitter and healthier with every stride. But for me it's about so much more than that – it's really about the mental clarity. Time away from my desk, my phone, my car, means that I'm all alone with my thoughts, and that's invaluable in my decision-making process.

I like to run first thing, because that means I can close my eyes and feel restful when my head hits the pillow the night before; I know that I'll have time and space at the start of the day to work through whatever issues are preoccupying me. It's double bubble for me: a better sleep the night before because I know what's coming in the morning, and a better sleep the night after thanks to the exercise itself.

During lockdown, my morning runs quickly became a coping mechanism for the stress of running the company, caring for the kids and keeping it all together for my loved ones. In the lighter mornings of early summer 2020 I was getting up earlier for the cherished hour to myself before the working and family days began. By breakfast time I was back home and wide awake.

I don't run fast or compete with myself for times and distances. Quite often I don't take a phone or device at all. As a result, if I'm simply enjoying the fresh air and the head space, I can do 10k without realizing, and I suspect that's because it's a space in my life where I'm not being ambitious or competitive. With the pressure to go further or go faster removed, I often find myself doing it anyway, but for the sheer joy of it rather than anything else.

Although lockdown and my time on *Strictly* has ended, running is a habit left over from those chaotic times that I have managed to keep up. Recently I had a huge meeting that would once have meant several sleepless nights beforehand as I'd try to thrash through the big decisions we'd be making. But setting my alarm for 5 a.m. helped me to get to sleep quicker as I spent less time tossing and turning, knowing I would have the time and space to make those big decisions in the morning with a clear head and a generous helping of endorphins. It doesn't matter what's providing these

Sara Davies

endorphins (within reason!), it's just about finding a healthy way for you to feel good about yourself so you can give your best to your business.

The Takeaway

Taking time to take care of your health can be the best investment that you make – not only will it give you more energy, but it allows you time to reset, refocus and re-energize. You don't have to run a marathon or climb a mountain; it's the act of taking time out to focus on your body that's the important part. To make this work for you:

- Build time into your schedule to exercise – it doesn't have to be intense, just regular.
- Use the time to allow your mind to drift. You may find you completely switch off from work for thirty minutes or spend the time planning your next big idea – your brain will choose what it needs time to do.

The Task

This week's task will depend on what you're already doing! If you already find the time to exercise regularly (two to three times per week, minimum) then I want you to write a list of the benefits that you feel it gives you. Ideally the list should have at least ten benefits on it. Then stick this to your fridge door – I'm not asking you to diet, just to remind yourself regularly of why you do what you do!

For those of you that don't currently exercise regularly, I want you to commit to three sessions of thirty minutes' exercise per week. You can choose whatever you think is achievable – a walk, a yoga class, a run, swimming . . . the list is endless.

Keep a diary of how you feel both before and after exercise, and keep it up for at least six weeks – yes, six weeks, because that's how long it takes for habits (good or bad) to become rooted in your behaviour.

66

Sara says:

It's easy to make excuses not to exercise, but think of exercise as a reward not a punishment – after all, you're investing in yourself, and that's important!

99

Lesson 52
It's Never Too Late to Start

Let Kamala be a lesson to all of us.

THE STORY

For our final lesson, I would like to tell you about my good friend and colleague Kamala, someone who I worked with almost from day one. As you'll remember from Lesson 12, she's the mam of my old schoolmate Meera, who called me out of the blue when my business was just starting.

The Vijayaraghavans are a very traditional Indian family – Meera's dad was a doctor and her mam had long been expected to stay at home and look after the family. Only by now, Meera and her brother had graduated from university and left home, leaving Kamala at home with not much to do, getting increasingly low and lonely.

There wasn't that much of a company structure back then, but the minute she came in it was obvious that Kamala was smart and a hard-worker. To start with, she was packing up orders, and occasionally she was answering the phone – only we had no real team yet, so she would answer the phone with 'Hello, Crafter's Companion. Can I help?', before replying to the person's request with, 'Sure, I'll just check if there's anyone in accounts/customer services/production available,' before putting her hand over the receiver and walking across the room to pass the phone to me while mouthing which department I was meant to be.

I'm not telling you all this to dazzle you with how lo-fi our operation started out, but to remind you that Kamala wasn't just our first-ever employee, she was doing a salaried job for the first time in her life, and she built up to having a place on our board of directors, running our company bank accounts.

So if you're sitting there on the train or the sofa, book in hand, feeling overwhelmed by the amount to do or the fact that you've never done any of this before, I'd like you to remember Kamala. Kamala who only entered the workforce once her kids had grown up and left home; Kamala who so quickly found a way to shine even without decades of work experience behind her. Kamala became a key player in a big company that has greatly benefited from her part in it.

Even if it seems too late to start a business, change your career or move to a new job, it never is. You'll be bringing a vast amount of life experience to your new role and you'll have the benefit of hindsight about so many things. Today is a fine time to start. And you have the example of Kamala's inspiring career trajectory. So put aside any feelings of being overwhelmed or of self-doubt and remember Kamala – and that it is never too late.

The Takeaway

The fact that you're reading this book means that you already have an itch to do something – it might be something new, it might be something challenging, it might be something downright remarkable. So, here's my next piece of advice:

- Don't ignore the itch – scratch it!

The Task

First of all, I want you to give yourself a pat on the back, because all the signs are that if you're reading this, then we've already been on a journey together!

This week is an opportunity to reflect: what has changed within your business or your work life since we began this journey? What has changed within you?

And what single piece of advice have you found most useful? Drop me a note direct – I'd love to hear from you. You can email me at: sara@sixminuteentrepreneur.com

> 66
>
> *Sara says:*
>
> **Starting a journey can be the hardest part, but if you never start, you'll never know. Don't wait: do it now!**
>
> 99

Epilogue

If you've reached this epilogue (without skipping through any of the lessons!), you should now have the mindset, the tools and the takeaways to lead a business with passion, vision and drive. As well as that, I hope that some of my stories about past mistakes, personal challenges and personnel challenges have helped to illustrate how much we can do when we set our mind to it.

But remember, setting up your own business or developing your career is an ongoing project. So, you can come back to any of these lessons and takeaways whenever you need to – whether it's for a splash of inspiration, a reminder of what you're capable of, or even just a giggle at some of my own disasters or motivation from my triumphs.

Reading the advice of my business mentors transformed the trajectory of my career when I was just starting out, and these days talking and mentoring the next generation of business minds is one of my favourite parts of my role. So, I do hope that this book helps you, whatever stage you're at. Good luck, and may you succeed in whatever you set out to achieve.

About the Author

Sara Davies MBE is the youngest ever female investor to appear on BBC One's *Dragons' Den* and is well known as the founder and creative director of the successful craft business Crafter's Companion. Launched while Sara was still at university, Crafter's Companion is now a global business selling papercraft, art, needlecraft and stationery items across forty countries.